THE LETTERS OF THOMAS GAINSBOROUGH

The Letters of Thomas GAINSBOROUGH

Edited by

MARY WOODALL

C.B.E., PH.D., F.S.A., F.M.A.

NEW YORK GRAPHIC SOCIETY

Greenwich, Connecticut

First printed in a limited edition of 400 copies for Subscribers only by the Lion and Unicorn Press at the Royal College of Art, London, in 1961.

The text of this revised edition, limited to 1200 copies, has been printed in Great Britain by Percy Lund, Humphries & Co. Ltd at the Country Press, Bradford. The collotype plates have been printed in Great Britain by the Chiswick Press. The book has been bound by James Burn & Co. Ltd.

LIST OF ILLUSTRATIONS

1727   24th May, baptized Sudbury Suffolk fifth son of John Gainsborough, cloth merchant, and Mary Burrough.

1740   Sent to London to study, worked with Gravelot, remained there until 1748.

1746   Married Margaret Burr, 15th July.

1748   Birth of elder daughter Mary. Returned to Sudbury, and soon after this settled in Ipswich.

1752   Birth of second daughter Margaret.

1753   Met Philip Thicknesse, Governor of Landguard Fort, who was his first biographer.

1759   Moved to Bath, October.

1761   First sent a portrait (Lord Nugent) for exhibition at the Society of Artists, London.

1763   First sent a landscape to Society of Artists.

1766   Moved to a house in the Circus, Bath.

1768   Invited to become a founder-member of the Royal Academy.

1769   Exhibited at first Royal Academy.

1772   His nephew Gainsborough Dupont apprenticed to him.

1774   Moved to London – settled in part of Schomberg House, Pall Mall.

1777   First supported by Henry Bate-Dudley in the press.

1780   His daughter Mary married Johann Christian Fischer.

1781   First patronised by the Royal Family.

1782   Sir Joshua bought "Girl with Pigs".

1783   Sketching expedition to the Lakes.

1784   Quarrelled with Royal Academy and withdrew his pictures, hereafter he showed his pictures annually at Schomberg House.

1788   2nd August, died and was buried at Kew.

My thanks are due to all those who have so kindly allowed me to reproduce letters and pictures. I am especially grateful to Professor E. K. Waterhouse for so much information and advice in preparing this book and for the loan of photographs. I should also like to thank Mr. Robert Wark of the Henry E. Huntingdon Library, who brought to my notice several unpublished letters from collections in the U.S.A.; the editors of the *Burlington Magazine*, and the *Connoisseur* for permission to reproduce letters and all the librarians and other persons who have facilitated my researches.

Wherever possible I have transcribed the original manuscript or photostats of the letters. In other cases I have taken them from the earliest published versions, unfortunately neither Fulcher nor Whitley gave the sources of the letters they publish. In general I have used the writer's capitalisation and spelling, but I have in a few cases altered the punctuation when so erratic as not to make sense. In one or two instances the sense of the letters is obscure but I have thought it better to print the words as they are in the original and not to attempt any elucidation.

In order to avoid repetition I have used abbreviations for my three main sources of reference as follows:

FULCHER =Fulcher, George William, *Life of Thomas Gainsborough, R.A.*, London, 1856, Second Edition.

WHITLEY =Whitley, William T., *Thomas Gainsborough*, London, 1915.

E.K.W. =Waterhouse, Ellis K., *Gainsborough*, London, 1958. This contains a fairly full Gainsborough bibliography. Most of the references in my notes are to the numbers in his catalogue, the page references are to his Introduction.

In an article published in the *Morning Herald* shortly after Gainsborough's death Sir Henry Bate-Dudley wrote: "His epistolary correspondence possessed the ease of Swift and the nervous force of Bolingbroke, and a selection of his letters would offer the world as much originality and beauty as is ever to be traced in his paintings..."[1] A further tribute is found in *Notes & Queries* for February, 1895, where the writer, who signs himself Lostwithiel, says "Jackson of Exeter says of those letters that, but for their manifest originality they might be said to be modelled on Sterne's. They have never been published. It is to be hoped they are not lost—all his remarks are brilliant and happy. Is it possible now to collect these letters?" This volume is in part the answer; it has been possible to collect about eighty letters, but many must have been lost since Gainsborough was a natural letter-writer who probably carried on a voluminous correspondence.

William Jackson, who was a composer and organist of Exeter Cathedral, was the recipient of many letters from Gainsborough, and well qualified to appraise them; in his character of the painter, he says "Gainsborough avoided the company of literary men—who were his aversion he was better pleased to give than to receive information ... so far from writing he scarcely ever read a book—but, for a letter to an intimate friend, he had few equals, and no superior. It was like his conversation gay, lively and fluttering round subjects which he just touched and away to another—expressing his thoughts with so little reserve that his correspondents, considering the letter as part of their friend had never the heart to burn it.[2]" What higher praise than that a letter be part of a friend!

1 Whitley, W. T., *An Eighteenth Century Art Chronicler, Sir Henry Bate Dudley; Walpole Society*, Vol. XIII, *p.* 60

2. Jack, William, of Exeter, *The Four Ages together with Essays on Various Subjects*, London, 1798, *p.* 183

The greater number of the surviving letters have been published and are scattered amongst Gainsborough literature, notably the series written to William Jackson and now in the possession of the Royal Academy; and those to James Unwin, Gainsborough's attorney and friend, published in the *Connoisseur* in 1922, many of which are now in the British Museum. But there is a number in private possession and in public collections, which have so far been accessible only to students. If any excuse is needed for republishing so much material it is that only when the letters are read together do they make an immediate impact. They speak for themselves and present the writer's character more vividly than is possible for any biographer.

Gainsborough reveals himself as a lovable and warm hearted man, devoted to his family and to his many friends. Full of enthusiasms he expressed himself in sprightly staccato phrases with a sparkling wit, but his moods varied greatly, and elation gave way to depression in quick succession. He changed his key from jocular to serious from sentence to sentence and although an incurable joker, he was always good humoured. In one of his most interesting letters written to Prince Hoare, in which he discusses Reynolds' theories about history painting, he concludes by saying of himself "Mr. G. hates of all things the least tendency to the sour Critic."

Testimony to Gainsborough's good manners is provided by Sarah Kirby when she wrote to congratulate her brother William on being placed to study under him. "Having so good an example to copy after", she says, "I imagine you improve very much in politeness.[1]" Some writers seem to have thought the intimate letters to Jackson contained coarse expressions, but I have found nothing that seems exceptionable and have printed them in full. The letters to Kilderbee may have been broader since according to a contemporary account they were "brilliant but eccentric and too licentious to be published.[2]"

1 Fulcher, *p.* 41   2 Whitley, *p.* 58

They have apparently disappeared and may have been destroyed by
Kilderbee's heirs.

The letters to his friend and attorney James Unwin were published by Sydney E. Harrison, in the *Connoisseur* in January and February, 1922, together with drafts for payments and Unwin's accounts under the title *New Light on a Gainsborough Mystery*. The Unwin accounts prove that the source of the annuity paid to the artist was a charge on the estate of the Duke of Beaufort and suggest that Mrs. Gainsborough was the illegitimate daughter of the fourth Duke, which is borne out by her hints at royal blood in her veins. Unwin clearly acted as one of Gainsborough's bankers as well as his attorney but was also an intimate friend. Unwin had to know of Gainsborough's peccadillos, which he confesses with engaging frankness promising to improve his ways. He tells Unwin a good deal of his life in Bath, and of the way in which the town was developing and makes some revealing comments about his wife and little daughters. He had been ill and writes "My Dear Good Wife has sat up every night til within a few, and has give me all the Comfort that was in her power. I shall never be a quarter good enough for her if I mend a hundred degrees." It is clear from one of his letters to his sister Mrs. Gibbon that his wife was not the ideal companion: "If I tell you my wife is weak but good, and never much formed to humour my Happiness, what can you do to alter her?" Gainsborough was an affectionate father and asking that his wife and dear girls should be remembered to Mrs. Unwin says "They are thank God charmingly well and whats more (tho' I say it) good in grain." He was anxious that his daughters should be properly taught. "I'm upon a scheme of learning them both to paint Landscape and that somewhat above the common Fan mount style. I don't mean to make them only Miss Fords in the Art, to be partly admired and partly laughed at at every Tea Table." Miss Ford, afterwards Mrs. Philip Thicknesse, fancied herself at the Viol da Gamba and often displayed her talents at social gatherings.

The majority of the existing letters to members of his family are to his sister Mrs. Gibbon for whom he had a strong brotherly affection, although he sometimes laughed at her non-conformist principles. In a letter to Dr. Charlton in which he announces his intention of presenting him with a picture he says, "I'd give it to Mother Gibbon but she delights not in worldly Prospects; I have a d—mned plague with Her when she comes to Town, to find out new Methodist Chapels enough for Her, for she Prays double sides, and cares not a farthing for what Bishops can say." But he confided his family troubles to her:"If I complain that Peggy is a sensible good Girl, but Insolent and proud in her behaviour to me at times, can you make your arm long enough to box her ears for me whilst you live at Bath? And (what hurt me most of late) were I to unfold a secret and tell you that I have detected a sly trick in Molly by a sight I got of one of her Letters, forsooth, to Mr. Fischer—what could all your cleverness do for me there? and yet I wish for your Head-piece to catch a little more of the secret." Gainsborough was referring to the clandestine love affair with the oboe player Fischer. He advised Mary strongly against the marriage, as he knew it would not be happy, but he was obliged to acquiesce and his forebodings were sadly justified, the young couple only lived a few months together. Gainsborough was fond of his brother Humphrey and writes sympathetically of him to Mrs. Gibbon. John the other brother mentioned in the correspondence seems to have been somewhat of a trial being very impractical about his financial affairs, and Gains-borough who was usually generous only allowed his brother half a crown a week, which was dispensed through his sister, Mrs. Dupont.

His friends were musicians, actors and painters,and it was these he loved to paint; there were few literary characters among his sitters. He hated gentlemen—advising Jackson against them he said:"Damn Gentlemen, there is not such a set of Enemies to a real artist in the world as they are, if not kept at a proper distance. *They* think (and so may you for a while) that they reward your merit by their Company & notice; but I who blow away all the chaff & by G— in their eyes too if they dont stand clear, know that they have but one part worth looking at, and that is their Purse."

Gainsborough was passionately fond of music, and in writing of painting he often used musical comparisons. He was intimate with most of the distinguished musicians in England, and amongst others painted Abel, J. C. Bach, Giardini and Fischer. Angelo describes meetings at his house when Bach and Abel together with Cipriani, Bartolozzi and others met and amused themselves with drawing, music and conversation long after midnight. Gainsborough must often have been there and he tried his hand at a number of instruments; he was eager to try Giardini's fiddle or Abel's Viol da Gamba thinking that by that means he might produce the same music as they. But although the evidence is conflicting, it does not seem that he was a very fine performer. John Christian Bach was exasperated when he called on Gainsborough in Pall Mall and found him playing the bassoon, "Pote it away, man; pote it away", he shouted, "do you want to burst yourself, like the frog in the fable.[1]"

There is little doubt, however, that Gainsborough was very sensitive to music. In a letter to Cipriani he writes of musical evenings in London just before he moved from Bath. "I have done nothing but fiddle since I came from London, so much was I unsettled by the continual run of Pleasure which my Friend Giardini and the rest of you engaged me in, and if it were not for my Family, which one cannot conveniently carry in one's Pocket, I should be often with you, enjoying what I like *up to the Hilt*." Abel was a particular friend of Gainsborough and his letter to Bate when Abel died is a moving tribute: "Poor Abel died about one o clock to-day. . . . We love a genius for what he leaves and we mourn him for what he takes away. . . . Poor Abel!—'tis not a week since we were gay together, and that

[1] Charles Sandford Terry, *John Christian Bach*, 1929, *p.* 93

he wrote the sweetest air I have in my collection of his happiest thoughts. My heart is too full to say more."

It was in the early years at Bath that Gainsborough met Garrick who was his valued friend until the actor's death in 1779. Fortunately a small group of letters to Garrick have survived and show Gainsborough's great affection for the actor and admiration of his art. Particularly interesting is the letter about the portrait of Garrick with the bust of Shakespeare, which eventually went to Stratford for the Festival of 1769. It throws some light on Gainsborough's attitude to portrait painting. "I was willing", he says, "like an Ass as I am, to expose myself a little out of the simple Portrait way, and had a notion of showing where that inimitable Poet had his Ideas from, by an immediate Ray darting down upon his Eye turn'd up for the purpose." Generally, Gainsborough was content to paint his sitters in a straightforward objective way relying for his effect on the study of their characters and the expressive handling of the paint. But on this occasion he was trying to enhance the picture by allusions which he could not realise; as he confesses later in the letter:"I must make a Plain Picture of Him standing erect & give it an old look."

Another actor friend was John Henderson, whom Gainsborough advised to learn from Garrick. "Garrick is the greatest creature living, in every respect; he is worth studying in every action. Every view, and every idea of him, is worthy of being stored up for imitation; and I have ever found him a generous and sincere friend. . . . ". This is emphasised by a remark in a second letter to Henderson. "Never mind the fools who talk of imitation and copying: all is imitation. . . . Why Sir what makes the difference between man and man, is real performance, and not genius or conception."

In reading Gainsborough's letters, students of his painting and drawing must be struck with the parallels between his writing and his pencilling on which he set so much store. Reynolds, in his fourteenth discourse, speaking of Gainsborough's manner of working, referred to "those odd scratches and marks which at a distance assume form", by which he meant, of course, Gainsborough's "hatching", that is the little brush strokes with which he built up his forms. The scratches and marks are echoed in the crisp and lively phrasing of the letters. Although Gainsborough says little about his actual technique there are revealing notes, in a letter to Mr. Edgar, the attorney at Colchester; "You please me much", he wrote, "by saying that no other fault is to be found in your picture than the roughness of the surface, for that part being of use in giving force to the effect at a proper distance, and what a judge of painting knows an original from a copy by; in short being the touch of the pencil which is harder to preserve than smoothness. I am much better pleas'd that they should spy out things of that kind, than to see an eye half an inch out of its place, or a nose out of drawing when viewed at a proper distance."

A letter to the Royal Academy of 1784 about the *Portrait of the Three Elder Princesses* again insists on the necessity to see pictures at a proper distance and in the proper light. Gainsborough had asked that the picture should be hung lower than the established line, which was about 8 feet from the ground. He writes in the third person:"as he has painted the Picture of the Princesses in so tender a light. . . . he cannot possibly consent to have it placed higher than five feet & a half because the likenesses & Work of the Picture will not be seen any higher." The authorities, however, found it impossible to comply with his request and he removed all his pictures from exhibition never again submitting any canvases. Ozias Humphrey who knew Gainsborough at Bath left some notes about his methods saying he began his portraits in a darkened room so that he might more easily see the whole before he was distracted by detail; it was only later that he let in more light and seems to have finished the head before completing the rest of the figure. In these letters Gainsborough's impressionistic technique is implied, and the detail of the portrait of *Three Princesses* (Pl. 2) shows this very clearly; it is even more evident in a late work *Diana and Actaeon* (Pl. 3). Gainsborough's point about the importance of the tactful hanging of his pictures is emphasised in another letter to the Royal Academy. He had sent the group of portraits of King George III and Queen Charlotte with their thirteen children, to the exhibition in 1781 and included in his letter is a sketch showing how they should be grouped, in three rows of five with the frames touching.

His letters confirm his love of landscape painting but he was always practical and knew he must paint portraits to make the pot boil. In a letter to Jackson he says—"remember that in mine [profession] a Man may do great things and starve in a Garret if he does not conquer his Passions and conform to the *Common Eye* in chusing that branch which *they* will encourage & pay for." In his early years his landscapes were more inventive than his portraits, but as his work developed both landscapes and portraits were equally considered as pictures in which the same fundamental problems had to be solved. Of the *Cornard Wood*, now in the National Gallery, he wrote to Henry Bate-Dudley in 1788—"It is in some respects a little in the *schoolboy stile* — but I do not reflect on this without a secret gratification; for as an early instance how strong my inclination stood for Landskip, this picture was actually painted at Sudbury in the year 1748; it was begun *before I left school;* — and was the means of my Father's sending me to London." He went to London in 1740 at the age of thirteen and we can only assume that some of the sketches for the final picture were made in the schoolboy years as the picture bears no mark of having been on the stocks for a long period. It is close in style to Dutch seventeenth century painting, and it is interesting to find Gainsborough writing to Mr. Harvey of Catton, in the last years of his life, when he was already dying . . . " 'tis odd how all the Childish passions hang about me in sickness, I feel such a fondness for my first imitations of little Dutch Landskips that I can't keep from working an hour or two of a Day though with a great mixture of bodily Pain—I am so childish I could make a Kite, catch Gold Finches, or build little Ships—''. Other evidence of the influence of Dutch painting is found in the letter to Dr. Charlton:"I forgot entirely that you had a copy of the little dutch spire of my Hand, 'tis not worth a farthing, so do what you please with it, hang it in the study at [?] where it may not be compared with the original.''

He is more formal when writing to Lord Hardwicke about 1764 with reference to a commission which he had evidently been offered to paint his Lordship's house and park. Beginning by expressing the honour done him he goes on to say . . . "but with respect to *real Views* from Nature in this Country he has never seen any Place that affords a Subject equal to the poorest imitations of Gaspar or Claude. Paul Sanby is the only Man of Genius, he believes, who has employ'd his Pencil that way. . . . if his Lordship wishes to have anything tolerable of the name of G, the subject altogether as well as figures etc. must be of his own Brain; otherwise Lord Hardwicke will only pay for Encouraging a Man out of his way and had much better buy a picture of some of the good Old Masters.'' Quite clearly Gainsborough was not interested in topography but in the composition of something analogous to an ideal landscape so much admired in his day, and this idea is repeated in one of his letters to Jackson who had been recommending him to attempt a history picture; Gainsborough replies:"do you really think that a regular Composition in the Landskip way should ever be fill'd with History, or any figures but such as fill a place (I won't say stop a Gap) or to create a little business for the Eye to be drawn from the Trees in order to return to them with more glee.''

Both these letters show that Gainsborough was not directly inspired by Nature as was John Constable, who claimed to have learnt so much from him. He is known to have made many sketches in pencil, chalks and oils, probably working from nature, but to arrive at a "composition in the landscape way" he made great use of models, building up landscapes from sticks and stones, broccoli and corks, lighting them from various angles with candles from which he made drawings in the evenings. But although he used these studies as the architecture of his picture Gainsborough was greatly affected by Nature and the word painting in the famous letter to Jackson has a delightful freshness of vision—"I'm sick of Portraits and wish very much to take my Viol da Gamba and walk off to some sweet Village when I can paint Landskips and enjoy the fag End of Life in quietness and ease. . . . I hate a dust, the Kicking up of a dust, and being confined *in Harness* to follow the track, whilst others ride in the waggon, under cover, stretching their Legs in the straw at Ease, and gazing at Green Trees & Blue skies without half my *Taste*."

A letter to Garrick written in 1768 shows a new awareness of Rubens as a landscape painter. "I could wish you call *upon any pretence*. . . . at the Duke of Montagu, because you'd see the Duke and Duchess in my *last* manner; but not as if you thought anything of mine worth that trouble, only to see his Grace's Landskip of Rubens." A greater richness of colour and freedom in handling at this time may well have resulted from this experience. Towards the end of his life his facility of invention in composing landscapes developed and various new ideas were evolved; a group of sea pieces which recall Dutch painting; a number of views of cottages with peasants grouped round the door, which suggest a townsman's nostalgia for the country, and also a series of pictures which seem to be inspired by the wild mountain scenes of Salvator Rosa and Gaspar Poussin. One of these was exhibited at the Royal Academy in 1783, and in developing this "genre" Gainsborough evidently felt the necessity to refer directly to nature and to make drawings in mountain country because in 1783 he wrote to his friend William Pearce . . . "I don't know if I told you that I'm going along with a Suffolk friend to visit the Lakes in Cumberland and Westmoreland, and purpose, when I come back to show you that your Grays and Dr. Brownes are tawdry fan-painters. I purpose to mount all the Lakes in the next Exhibition in the great stile, and you know, if the people don't like them, 'tis only jumping into one of the deepest of them from off a wooded island, and my respectable reputation will be fixed for ever."

Although Jackson says he hated reading, Gainsborough confesses in one of his letters to a great interest in one of Sir Joshua's discourses, which had been shown to him by Mr. Hoare, "which he thinks amazingly clever, and cannot be too much admired (together with the Ingenious Author) by every candid lover of the Art. The truth of what he observes concerning Fresco, and the Great style, Mr. G. is convinced of by what he has often heard Mr. Hoare say of the works of Rafaelle and Michel Angelo—But betwixt Friends Sir Joshua either forgets, or does not chuse see that his Instruction is all adapted to form the History Painter, which he must know there is no call for in this country." He goes on to comment on Reynolds' so called ornamental style which the President considered a lower branch of art than history painting, and formed for portraits. Gainsborough says "he had better come *down to Watteau* at once (who was a very fine Painter taking away the french conceit). . . . Every one knows that the grand style must consist in plainess & simplicity, and that silks & satins, Pearls and trifling ornaments would be as hurtfull to simplicity, as flourishes in a Psalm Tune; but Fresco would no more do for Portraits than an Organ would please Ladies in the hands of Fischer; there must be variety of lively touches and surprizing Effects to make the Heart dance, or else they had better be in a Church—so in Portrait Painting there must be a Lustre and finishing to bring it up to individual Life." When Jackson suggested Gainsborough should paint history he retorts: "But are you sure you don't mean instead of the flight into Egypt, my flight out of Bath! Do you consider my dear maggotty Sir, what a deal of work history Pictures require to what little dirty subjects of coal horses & jackasses and such figures as I fill up with." Although he did not choose to use the accepted classical repertoire of the history painters, Gainsborough had a real understanding of the principles of composition in pictures, and there is little doubt that he studied the Old Masters, particularly in his latter years. There is an illuminating passage in one of the letters to Jackson . . . "The lugging in objects whether agreeable to the whole or not is a sign of the least Genius of anything, for a person able to collect in the mind will certainly groupe in the mind also . . . One part of a Picture ought to be like the first part of a Tune; that you can guess what follows, and that makes the second part of the Tune . . ."

In the letter already quoted to Prince Hoare on Reynolds' Discourses, discussing the great and ornamental styles, Gainsborough wrote about the things he loved to paint in portraits, silks and satins, pearls and flourishes. The shimmer of light moving on draperies and the fluttering of ribbons meant as much to him as the face and he contrived to make pictures of them when he was not greatly interested in the faces. It is always said that unlike his contemporaries he never used drapery painters, but he advises Jackson: "There is a branch of Painting next in profit to Portrait and quite in your power without any more drawing than I'll answer for your having, which is Drapery & Landskip backgrounds."

Gainsborough prided himself greatly on his power of getting a likeness and in this connection the letters to Lord Dartmouth are of considerable interest. Lord Dartmouth had evidently written that Lady Dartmouth's portrait was not like, and Gainsborough replied that he was willing to make alterations and believed the reason for the failure was the fact that he painted her in fancy dress. "I dont know" he asks, "if your Lordship remembers a few *impertinent* remarks of mine upon the ridiculous use of fancied Dresses in Portraits about the time that Lord North made us laugh in describing a *Family Piece* His Lordship had seen somewhere. . . . I will venture to say that had I painted Lady Dartmouths Picture dressed as her Ladyship goes, no fault (more than in my Painting in general) would have been found with it." Lord Dartmouth apparently replied with good humour, but Gainsborough thought he might think he was trying to save himself the trouble of painting another picture. He pointed out that he wanted to make an experiment showing the effect in changing the dress, but in order to do this he says "I must know if Lady Dartmouth Powders or not in common." The third letter is perhaps the most interesting in revealing Gainsborough's ideas—"Nothing", he says, "can be more absurd than the foolish custom of painters dressing people like Scaramouches, and expecting the likeness to appear. Had a picture voice, action, etc. to make itself known as Actors have upon the Stage, no disguise would be sufficient to conceal a person; . . . . I defy any but a Painter of some sagacity . . . . to be well aware of the different Effects which one part of a picture has upon another, and how the Eye may be cheated as to the appearance of size, and by an artful management of the accompanyments. A Tune may be so confused by a false Bass—that is if it is ever so plain, simple and full of meaning, it shall become a jumble of nonsense." He goes on to say he has more respect for truth than the finest invention and finally:"Lady Dartmouth's Picture will look more like and not so large when dressed properly." The two portraits are illustrated (Pl. 11 and 12). It seems fairly clear that Pl. 12 is the first portrait as the dress derives more or less from Van Dyck with the sleeves puffed and split open and trimmed with pearls. Almost all the eighteenth century portrait painters sometimes dressed their sitters to some degree in masquerade dress and it seems Lady Dartmouth was devoted to this idea. The other picture shows her in a contemporary négligé or dressing gown, and the high powdered hairdressing is rather later in date than that in the other picture.

This is not the place to discuss the use of masquerade dress in English portrait painting of the eighteenth century, a subject which will repay further research, but Gainsborough testifies to the practice in referring to Lord North's remarks about a "family piece he had seen somewhere" where the figures were in fancy dress. In this connection it is amusing to find Horace Walpole writing to Mann in 1741: "I saw at the Duchess of Norfolk's quantities of pretty Van Dyck's and all kinds of pictures walked out from their frames." Further light on the use of Van Dyck costume is found in a letter of 1734 from Sarah Duchess of Marlborough to her grand-daughter Diana Duchess of Bedford whose portrait she was commissioning from Isaac Whood. "Many women", she says, "are now drawn in the Van Dyck manner" and suggested that it should be modelled on Van Dyck's portrait of Anne Carr[1]. Diana objected that she would look old fashioned alongside of a recent portrait of her husband in Coronation robes, and Sarah thought Whood might compromise by imitating the white satin in Van Dyck's portrait but altering the sleeves and waist to bring it more up to date. This seems to be just the kind of thing which Gainsborough tried to do in the first portrait of Lady Dartmouth and in many of his portraits there are variants on Van Dyck dress which would hardly be recognised as such by seventeenth century dressmakers.[2]

Gainsborough's portraits proclaim him a discerning student of character,which is confirmed by a pen-portrait of Dunning written to Jackson—"In my way home I met with Ld Shelburne, who insisted on my making them a short visit, and I don't regret going ('tho I generally do to all Lord's Houses) as I met with Mr. Dunning there. There is something exclusive of the clear and deep understanding of that Gentleman most exceedingly pleasing to me—He seems the only man who talks as Giardini plays. . . . He is an amazing *compact* Man in every respect . . . his Store-Room seems cleared of all french

1 *Letters of a Grandmother* (1732–35), edited by Gladys Scott Thomson, 1943, *p.* 121

2 For further information on Vandyke Dress in the eighteenth century *see* J. L. Nevinson, *Vogue of the Vandyke Dress, Country Life Annual,* 1959, *p.* 25

ornaments and gingerbread work, everything is simplicity and elegance & in its proper place; no disorder or confusion in the *furniture* as if he was going to remove." He speaks of Dunning as "almost motionless, with a Mind brandishing like Lightening."

Gainsborough seems often to have been very dilatory in finishing his portraits, and in two cases he excuses himself most amusingly. To Unwin he writes:"Believe me my dear Friend, I'm most horribly ashamed of myself—come to see you indeed . . . I should blush if I thought you could ever spy me through a Telescope within the distance of a whole County of you." He is equally apologetic and witty in letters to Mr. Stevens and Mr. Stratford.

In this short introduction I have made no attempt to discuss Gainsborough's Art except in the context of the letters. It is not always easy to decipher his thoughts, which one suspects are often the inspiration of the moment, sometimes to be discarded later and not to be taken too seriously in building up his philosophy. But if he was not a profound thinker, he was full of common sense and real independence in his judgments. His writing, like his painting, is instinctive rather than scholarly, but the hastily composed phrases are often full of wisdom. He would have had little sympathy for the elegant letter writing of the eighteenth century and wrote as he would have talked—thinking aloud.

THE LETTERS OF THOMAS GAINSBOROUGH

From the original at the Royal Academy

1 The portraits of King George III and Queen Caroline and their thirteen children painted in September 1782 and shown at the R.A. 1783

2 "Three quarters" refers to the size of the canvas, i.e., 30×25 in. and not to a three quarter length portrait

From the original at the Royal Academy

1 Francis Milner Newton (1720–94) the first Secretary to the Royal Academy

2 Below the letter is a sketch showing how Gainsborough wished the Royal Portraits to be hung in three rows of five, the frames all touching

3 *Two Shepherd Boys with Dogs Fighting* (*Pl.* 9), *see E.K.W. p.* 800 and letter to Sir William Chambers, *p.* 43

4 Either the Mountain landscape belonging to Lord Sutherland, *see E.K.W.* 966, or the landscape in Philadelphia, *see E.K.W.* 968

5 *A view at the mouth of the Thames* (*Pl.* 4), now in Melbourne National Gallery, *see E.K.W.* 964

1 *The Three Elder Princesses* (*Pl.* 2) painted in 1784 to the order of the Prince of Wales for the State room at Carlton House where a frame had been built to receive it in one of the panels at a height of 5 ft. 5½ in. The picture is now at Windsor Castle, *see Whitley p.* 213 and *E.K.W.* 135.

2 It was the rule at Somerset House to hang full length portraits above the level of the doorways so that the base of the frames would be about 8 or 9 ft. from the floor. The authorities failed to comply with Gainsborough's request and the pictures were withdrawn; he never again sent to the Royal Academy

1. TO THE COUNCIL OF THE ROYAL ACADEMY

Mr. Gainsborough presents his compliments to the Gentlemen appointed to hang the pictures at the Royal Academy; and begs leave to *hint* to them, that if the Royal Family,[1] which he has sent for this Exhibition (*being smaller than three quarters*)[2] are hung above the line along with full-lengths, he never more, whilst he breaths, will send another picture to the Exhibition. This he swears by God. Saturday Morn.

[*April 1783*]

2. TO F. M. NEWTON[1]

Dear Newton, I wd beg to have them hung with the Frames touching each other, in this order.[2] The Names are written behind each Picture. God bless you hang my Dogs[3] and my Landskip[4] in the great Room. The sea Piece[5] you may fill the small Room with.

Yrs sincerely in haste

[*1783*]

T. GAINSBOROUGH

3. TO THE GENTLEMEN OF THE HANGING COMMITTEE OF THE ROYAL ACADEMY

Mr. Gainsborough's Compls to the Gentlemen of the Committee, and begs pardon for giving them so much trouble; but as he has painted the Picture of the Princesses,[1] in so tender a light, that notwithstanding he approves very much of the established Line[2] for strong Effects, he cannot possibly consent to have it placed higher than five feet & a half, because the likenesses & Work of the Picture will not be seen any higher; therefore at a word, he will not trouble the Gentlemen against their Inclination, but will beg the rest of his Pictures back again. Saturday Evening.

[*10th April, 1784*]

This is a copy of a letter from Gainsborough in the Royal Academy Council Minutes for the 9th April, 1784. The following note was sent in reply

"Sir

In compliance with your resquest the Council have ordered your Pictures to be taken down to be delivered to your order, whenever send for them

I am and etc.

Saturday evening 9 o/clo."

[*10th April, 1784*]

Taken from *Whitley p.* 282

1 The Reverend Henry Bate (1745–1824) afterwards Sir Henry Bate Dudley. In 1772 he helped to found the *Morning Post* of which he was editor, later he left it to establish the *Morning Herald.* From 1772 onwards he continually supported Gainsborough in the press. For a full account of him *see Whitley, Chap.* VII and W. T. Whitley, *Sir Henry Bate-Dudley, an Eighteenth Century Art Chronicler, Walpole Society, Vol.* XIII, *p.* 59, *et seq.*

2 Karl Frederick Abel (1725–87) the celebrated virtuoso on the Viol da Gamba, came to England in 1759. He was appointed one of the Chamber Musicians in the Queen's band and after 1762 he gave a series of concerts with J. C. Bach. According to Angelo* he completely covered the walls of his rooms with Gainsborough's drawings which the painter gave him in exchange for music. Gainsborough painted his portrait several times, *see E.K.W.* 1–3 *and pl.* 6.

* *Reminiscences of Henry Angelo*, Kegan Paul, London, 1904, *p.* 146

The original letter from Gainsborough seems to have disappeared but there is at the Royal Academy a sheet with sketches of eight of the pictures see Pl. 5. They are titled in Gainsborough's hand the Three Princesses, Lord and Lady Buckingham see E.K.W. *90 and 91,* Lord Rodney see E.K.W. *583,* Lord Rawdon see E.K.W. *353,* Two Boys with a dog, Masters Tomkinson see E.K.W. *667,* A half-length of Lord Hood see E.K.W. *376, and a* Family Picture, Mr. Bailey see E.K.W. *35.*

On the sheet Gainsborough has written:

"NB The Frame of the Princesses cannot be sent but with the picture as Their Majesties are to have a private view of the Picture at Buckingham House before it is sent to the Royal Academy"

and at the top of the sheet

"Portraits by T. Gainsborough, the frames sent."

Gainsborough has ticked in red ink, the two Buckingham portraits, Lord Rodney, Lord Rawdon, and the Tomkinson Boys and in the same ink has added the word come *to indicate that the pictures had been sent.*

4. TO HENRY BATE[1]

Poor Abel[2] died about one o'clock today, without pain, after three days sleep. Your regret, I am sure, will follow this loss. We love a genius for what he leaves and we mourn him for what he takes away. If Abel was not so great a man as Handel it was because caprice had ruined music before he ever took up the pen. For my part, I shall never cease looking up to heaven—the little while I have to stay behind—in hopes of getting one more glance of the man I loved from the moment I heard him touch the string. Poor Abel!—'tis not a week since we were gay together, and that he wrote the sweetest air I have in my collection of his happiest thoughts. My heart is too full to say more.

20th June 1787

32   Plate 1
THE MUSIC PARTY (DRAWING)
British Museum

Plate 2   33

DETAIL FROM THE THREE ELDER PRINCESSES
Reproduced by gracious permission of Her Majesty the Queen

C*

Taken from *Whitley p.* 298

1 Boydell, John (1719–1804), engraver, *c.* 1751 set up as a printseller and publisher of engravings. Commissioned well-known artists to paint pictures illustrating Shakespeare, and built the Shakespeare Gallery in Pall Mall to exhibit them. Boydell no doubt bought the Gainsborough landscape with a view to the engraving in aquatint by Mary Prestal published in 1790 (*see Whitley, p.* 299).

2 *The Cornard Wood*, now in the National Gallery, *see E.K.W.* 828.

From the original at Woburn

This letter from the Duke of Beaufort's agent is included here because it explains the two following letters

1 John, Fourth Duke of Bedford (1710–71). He presented his portrait (*Pl.* 8) to Trinity College, Dublin, when he was Chancellor of the University, 1768

The receipt is at Woburn, *viz.:*

Nov. 15th 1768

Rec[d] by His Grace The Duke of Bedford sixty Guineas, in full for a whole length Portrait of His Grace

—————— By me

£63 THO. GAINSBOROUGH

For other portraits of the Duke, *see E.K.W.* 53–57a

2 *See E.K.W.* 58

3 *See E.K.W.* 255

4 For copies and repetitions of Gainsborough's portraits, *see E.K.W. p.* 39

My Dear Sir, You have thanked me handsomely for what has not been handsomely done, but I intend you shall have something better soon.

Mr. Boydell[1] bought the large landscape[2] you speak of for seventy-five guineas last week at Greenwood's. It is in some respects a little in the *schoolboy stile*—but I do not reflect on this without a secret gratification; for as an early instance how strong my inclination stood for Landskip, this picture was actually painted at Sudbury in the year 1748; it was begun *before I left school*;—and was the means of my Father's sending me to London.

It may be worth remark that though there is very little idea of composition in the picture, the touch and closeness to nature in the study of the parts and *minutiae* are equal to any of my latter productions. In this explanation I do not wish to seem vain or ridiculous, but do not look on the Landskip as one of my riper performances.

It is full forty years since it was first delivered by me to go in search of those who had *taste* to admire it! Within that time it has been in the hands of twenty picture dealers, and I once bought it myself during that inverval for *Nineteen Guineas*. Is not that curious?— Yours, my dear Sir, most sincerely,

THOMAS GAINSBOROUGH

Pall Mall, March 11, 1788

6. TO THOMAS GAINSBOROUGH FROM P. BEAUMONT ESQ.
AGENT TO THE DUKE OF BEDFORD

Sir,

From the expectations you gave me when I saw you before I left Bath in November, I supposed before this time you wo'd have sent home the Pictures you painted for the Duke[1] & Duchess of Bedford.[2]

Her Grace now directs me to acquaint you that she desires you will immediately send her Picture & that of Lady Mary Fitzpatrick's,[3] & that they need not wait for His Grace's Picture if you have not yet finished the Copies[4] you were to make of it, but if they are done that the original can be spared you will please to send it with the two beforementioned.

Her Grace orders me to add that if it is agreeable to you to come to London & will keep to your usual prices she will be answerable for its paying the expenses of the journey.

Bedford House Jany. 4 1765

From the original at Woburn
Below is a receipt, now at Woburn, presumably for one copy and for
the portraits of the Duchess and Lady Mary Fitzpatrick

Nov[r]. 5th 1764
Rec[d]. of His Grace The Duke of Bedford sixty three Pounds,
in full for Three Portraits

——

£63   THO. GAINSBOROUGH

——

It appears that the other copy was not delivered until November
1769, see receipt, now at Woburn below, *see* G. Scott Thompson, *The
Russells of Bloomsbury*, 1940, *p.* 240

Bath Novr. 23rd 1769
Rec[d]. of His Grace The Duke of Bedford forty Guineas for a
half length Portrait of His Grace, and ten shillings for a Case,
in full of all Demands

————

£42 – 10   THOS. GAINSBOROUGH

From the original at Woburn
1 Walter Wiltshire the west Country "Pickford" of the day who lived
at Shockerwick near Bath owned many pictures by Gainsborough
including *The Harvest Waggon* now in the Barber Institute, Birmingham
2 *See E.K.W.* 57
Printed below is the receipt now at Woburn

April 28th 1768
Rec[d]. of His Grace The Duke of Bedford twenty one pounds,
for a three quarter Portrait of His Grace, sent to Mrs.
Fortescue in Dublin

——

£21   THOS. GAINSBOROUGH

——

7. TO P. BEAUMONT ESQ.

Sir,

I received the favor of your Letter yesterday, and beg you will be so good to let Their Graces know that my not sending the Pictures sooner has been owing to some Difficulty of pleasing myself in the two Copies of His Grace; but that they shall all be finished and sent next week without fail to Bedford House. I should be much obliged if you would also acquaint The Duchess that 'tho' my Ill Health forbids my following Business in London (to which I have frequent invitations) Her Grace may nevertheless command me at any time to paint *any of The Family* there.

I am Sir

Your most obedient humble servant

THO. GAINSBOROUGH

Bath   Jan. 7th 1765

8. TO MR. BEAUMONT

Sir

I have packed up Their Graces Pictures to come by Wiltshire's flying waggon,[1] which sets out from hence on Sunday Evening and arrives at the White Horse Cellar, Piccadilly, on Wednesday Morning. I have directed them to be called for there by your order, & beg the favor of you to send some careful Servant for Them. The Copy of The Duke's picture[2] I have not been able to finish so as to send along with the Original, and was afraid of keeping them any longer after having orders to send them; But if Mrs. Fortiscue is in Town, should be obliged if you will acquaint Her that it shall be sent as soon as possible to Bedford House.

I am Sir

Your most obedient & obliged humble Servant

THO. GAINSBOROUGH

Bath Saturday Jan. 27th 1765

From the original at Woburn, *see The Correspondence of John, Fourth Duke of Bedford*, Vol. III, Longmans, 1846
1 For biography *see* under letters to William Jackson

Taken from *Whitley* unpublished papers British Museum; sold Sotheby 24th June, 1924, 295(7)
1 Robert Bowyer (1758–1834) the miniature painter, lived in Schomberg House after Gainsborough's death and there arranged an exhibition of pictures illustrating Hume's *History of England*, *see Whitley p.* 342
2 William Heberden the elder (1710–1801) physician, first described *Angina Pectoris*
3 John Hunter, F.R.S. (1728–93), author of a Treatise on the Blood, his scientific and art collections were bought by the Nation and acquired by the College of Surgeons in 1800

My Lord Duke   A most worthy honest Man, and one of the greatest Genius's for Musical Compositions England ever produced, is now in London, and has got two or three Members of Parliament along with him out of Devonshire, to make application for one of the Receivers of the Land-Tax for that County, now resign'd by a very old Man one Mr. Haddy—His name is William Jackson[1], lives at Exeter and for his plainness, truth and Ingenuity at the same time, is beloved as no man ever was. Your Grace has doubtless heard his Compositions but He is no *Fiddler* your Grace may take my word for it; he is extremely clever and good, is a married man with a young Family and is qualified over and over for the Place; has got Friends of Fortune who will be bound for him in any sum, and they are all making application to His Grace the Duke of Grafton to get him this Place—But, my Lord Duke, I told him they could not do it without me, that I must write to your Grace about it.

He is at Mr. Arnold's in Norfolk Street in the Strand, and if your Grace would be pleased to think of it, I should be ever bound to Pray for your Grace—Your Grace knows that I am an *Original* and therefore I hope will be the more ready to pardon this monstrous freedom from

> Your Grace's
> most dutiful most Grateful
> & obedient servant
> THO. GAINSBOROUGH

Bath May 29th. 1768

10. TO R. BOWYER[1]

I am extremely obliged to you for your kind anxiety for my recovery. But as I have reason and every assurance from Dr. Heberden[2] (who has known many swellings dispersed like mine and no mischief come) I shall not on any account interfere in what Mr. Hunter[3] is about.

1st May 1788

40

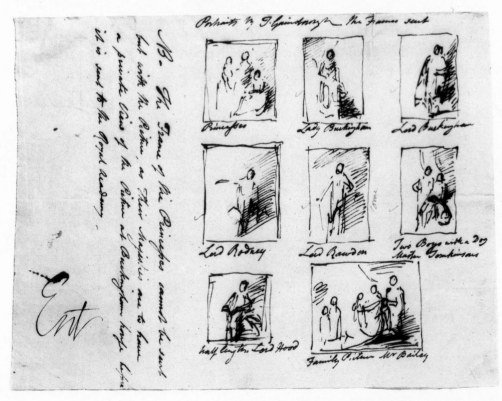

Plate 4
A VIEW AT THE MOUTH OF THE THAMES
National Gallery, Melbourne

Plate 5
A PAGE FROM A LETTER SHOWING SKETCHES OF EIGHT OF THE PICTURES
GAINSBOROUGH INTENDED SENDING TO THE ROYAL ACADEMY EXHIBITION
IN 1784

From *Whitley* unpublished papers British Museum; sold Sotheby 12th October, 1954 (170)

1 Chambers, Sir William (1723–96). Architect, author of two works which had a great influence on the architecture of the day, *Designs of Chinese Buildings* (1757), based on actual buildings seen in China, and *Treatise on Civil Architecture*. The ornamental buildings at Kew and Somerset House are amongst his best known works. He was the first Treasurer of the Royal Academy

2 *Two Shepherd Boys with Dogs Fighting* (*Pl.* 9), now in the Iveagh Bequest, Kenwood, London, *see E.K.W.* 800 and letter to Newton, *p.* 29

From the original in the Holburne of Menstrie Museum, Bath, *Pl.* 10

1 Dr. Rice Charlton (1710–89). His portrait by Gainsborough is in the Holburne of Menstrie Museum, Bath, *see E.K.W.* 136

11. TO SIR WILLIAM CHAMBERS, R.A.[1]

Dear Sir,

You'll perceive the danger of writing polite, friendly letters to me, as I am already about to ask a favour of you. My wife has a poor relation from Scotland, a Joiner, who for want of work in his own country has been obliged to leave a handsome wife & children behind him to seek employment in London. It has occurred to my good woman that as you must necessarily have a great number of hands at your *feet*, that you might perhaps be so good as to think of him when convenient. He is a good workman about thirty years of age, an honest, sober, hardworking creature.

I hear poor Newton is better, which I am honestly glad of; the world cannot supply his loss should he drop. I hope you had as cheerful a day yesterday as you could without him. I sent my fighting dogs[2] to divert you. I believe next exhibition I shall make the boys fighting & the dogs looking on—you know my cunning way of avoiding great subjects in painting & of concealing my ignorance by a flash in the pan. If I can do this while I pick pockets in the portrait way two or three years longer I intend to turn into a cot & turn a serious fellow; but for the present I must affect a little madness. I know you think me right as a whole, & can look down upon Cock Sparrows as a great man ought to do, with compassion.

> Believe me, my dear Sir
> Your lways obedient Humble Servant
> THOS. GAINSBOROUGH

Pall Mall, April 27th, 1783.

12. TO DOCTOR CHARLETON[1] AT WOODHOUSE NEAR BRISTOL

Dear Sir,

I must beg pardon for not answering your Letter sooner, I have had some plaguesome sitters, and a sick House besides, but thank God all is right again. Molly had a smart fever at the time I recd. your Letter, but my next door neighbour Doctor Heberden sent Her to Chiswick for Air, and now she is *purely* as my Friend Bob said to the old woman. I hope all your fears and apprehensions about Him are only signs of your feeling quicker and deeper than the generality of Parents, which you certainly do, and that His complaint is by this time removed. I'll trust you for taking Him under your Eye the

2 Mrs. Mary Gibbon, Gainsborough's sister, *see* letters to her

From the original in the possession of Mr. R. N. Carew Hunt in 1942, *see* R. Edwards, *Burl. Mag. p.* 152, June 1942

1 Cipriani, Giovanni Battista (1727–85) history and decorative painter came to London in 1755

2 Mr. Hamilton, probably Colonel James Hamilton, a Bath collector, to whom Gainsborough gave *The Boy at the Stile*, being so charmed with his violin playing, *see E.K.W.* 889

3 Giardini, Felice de (1716–96) Italian violinist and composer: played in the opera orchestras at Rome and Naples, in 1748 visited Germany and settled in England in 1750. His immense success on arrival may be attributed to the fact that he was the first violin virtuoso of eminence to be heard in England. He became leader of the opera orchestra in 1752. Played and taught in London until 1784 when he was eclipsed by rivals. He retired to Italy but returned to London in 1790, he died on a tour in Russia

moment He ailes anything and I think you right, for a stitch in time spares nine says Bobby's old woman—

My dear Doctor, I forgot entirely that you had a copy of the little dutch spire of my Hand, 'tis not worth a farthing, so do what you please with it, hang it in your study at [?] where it may not be compared with the original and I shall be easy; I'd give it to Mother Gibbon[2] but she delights not in worldly Prospects; I have a d—mned plague with Her when she comes to Town, to find out new Methodist Chapels enough for Her, for she Prays double sides, and cares not a farthing for what Bishops can say, so that some [?] swears that the whole work is already performed by *promises*.

I beg my best respects to your
Family and I am Dear Sir,
Your ever sincere & Obedt.
Serv't.

THOS. GAINSBOROUGH

Pall Mall, 24th June 1779.

Tell Bob He will certainly find a use for His Gun for the French intend landing at Bristol—don't you believe it yourself.

13. TO MR. CIPRIANI[1]

Dear Sir,

I should have done myself the pleasure of writing to you sooner but that I could not 'til yesterday get a sight of Mr. Hamilton[2] and his Pictures. I find that he reserved the two churches you mentioned for his House in the Crescent, and that no Price would tempt him to part with them. They are really very fine Pictures. I have done nothing but fiddle since I came from London, so much was I un-settled by the continual run of Pleasure which my Friend Giardini[3] and the rest of you engaged me in, and if it were not for my Family, which one cannot conveniently carry in one's Pocket, I should be often with you, enjoying what I like *up to the Hilt*. I hope that all our Friends are well towards the City?

I have wrote two Letters in the little time I have been at Home to Giardini, and the D—l a word can I draw from him, 'tho in my last I fudged up a pretence of wanting a tune which I left in his Parlour that Abel wrote for me, only to extract a word or two against his will. I'm cursedly afraid that I have afronted him with an old trick of mine, commonly called a hum, for you must know I took it into my

4 It has been suggested to me by Professor Waterhouse that the joke about the copy may indicate that Gainsborough Dupont, the artist's nephew, apprenticed to him in 1772, may already have been making copies of such pictures by his uncle. The reference to "ragged children" at this date is interesting since Gainsborough's known "fancy pictures" date from the eighties, *see E.K.W. p.* 35 *et. seq.*

5 Bartolozzi Francesco (1727–1815). Engraver, born Florence came to England in 1764 as engraver to the King; was an original member of the Royal Academy. Famous for his engravings after the old masters

From the original in the possession of Messrs. Myers in 1945

1 Richard Cosway (1740–1821) portrait painter in oils and Miniature painter, R.A. 1771. A collector and dealer in works of art. He lived next door to Gainsborough in Pall Mall

The meaning of this letter is obscure

Taken from the original in the possession of the Earl of Dartmouth on deposit at the William Salt Library, Stafford

1 For portraits of the Earl and Countess of Dartmouth, *see E.K.W.* 185 and 187

Head one Day as I was going in his Chariot with him to insinuate (merely to try his temper, and a damned trick it was) that the Picture he has of mine of the Cottage and ragged family was only a *Copy*.[4] I believe you can set him right about that, and he was cunning enough not to seem the least hurt. I repented as I generally do very soon after my folly, and the more so as he has always been the politest creature to me I ever was acquainted with. I wish my Dear Cip you would pump him a little and give me a line. I have a tollerable Picture of another rural subject which I entend for him but I would not have him know it.

I beg my best compliments [to] you [one word obliterated] and amiable Pupil and his fair Lady, and to Mr. Bartolozzi[5] when you see Him. I should heartily rejoyce to see you all at Bath and will do my utmost to make the Place agreable to you.

Believe me

Dear Sir

Yrs most truly,

THO. GAINSBOROUGH

Bath, Feb. 14, 1774.

> To Mr. Cipriani,
> Near the Mewes Gate Hedge Lane
> Charing Cross
> London.

14. TO MR. COSWAY[1]

Mr. Gainsborough presents his Compliments to Mr. Cosway; and as he finds there has been a loss of *Iron* betwixt us, he begs in case it must be repaired with *Gold or Silver*, that he may be permitted to share the expense with Mr. Cosway.

15. RECEIPT SENT BY GAINSBOROUGH TO THE EARL OF DARTMOUTH

Recd of the Rt. Honble Earl of Dartmouth, one hundred & twenty six pounds, in full for two half length portraits[1]

£126   THO. GAINSBOROUGH

May 25th 1769

This and the two following letters are published in the *Royal Commission on Historic MS.*, Vol. XV, *p.* 193, *et. seq.*

The first two are taken from the originals in the Collection of the Earl of Dartmouth on deposit at the William Salt Library, Stafford, and the last from the Royal Commission Volume; this last was sold at Sotheby, 24th June, 1924, 295 (1), its present location is unknown. There are two portraits of Lady Dartmouth in the collection of the Earl of Dartmouth, it seems that the letters refer to *Pl.* 12, this I am assured by Mrs. Eric Newton is not contemporary dress and derives more or less from Van Dyck with the sleeves puffed slit open and laced with pearls. Most of the English portrait painters in the eighteenth century at times dressed their sitters to some degree in masquerade dress, and it seems Lady Dartmouth was devoted to the idea. The other picture (*Pl.* 11) is probably Gainsborough's second version, as it shows her wearing a négligé or dressing gown which is in the contemporary fashion, and the high, powdered dressing of the hair is later in date than the fashion shown in the first portrait; *see* Introduction *p.* 23

My Lord

I recd the honour of your Lordships letter acquainting me that I am to expect Lady Dartmouth's Picture at Bath, but it is not yet arrived—I shall be extremely willing to make any alterations your Lordship shall require, when Her ladyship comes to Bath for that purpose, as I cannot (without taking away the likeness) touch it unless from the Life.

I would not be thought by what I am going to observe that I am at all unwilling to do anything your Lordship requires to it or even to paint an entire new picture for the money I received for that, as I shall always take pleasure in doing anything for Lord Dartmouth, but I should fancy myself a great blockhead if I was capable of painting such a Likeness as I did of your Lordship, and not have sense enough to see why I did not give the same satifaction in Lady Dartmouths Picture; & I believe your Lordship will agree with me in this point, that next to being able to paint a tollerable Picture, is having judgment enough to see what is the matter with a bad one. I don't know if your Lordship remembers a few *impertinent* remarks of mine upon the ridiculous use of fancied Dresses in Portraits about the time that Lord North made us laugh in describing a *Family Piece* His Lordship had seen somewhere, but whether your Lordship's memory will reach this trifling circumstance or not, I will venture to say that had I painted Lady Dartmouths Picture, dressed as her Ladyship goes, no fault (more than in my Painting in general) would have been found with it. Believe me, My Lord, 'tho I may appear conceited in saying it so confident^{ly}.

I never was far from the mark, but I was able before I pull'd the trigger to see the cause of my missing and nothing is so common with me as to give up my own sight in my Painting room rather than hazard giving offence to my best Customers. You see, my Lord, I can speak plainly when there is no danger of having my bones broke, and if your Lordship encourages my giving still a free opinion upon the matter, I will do it in another Line.

I am your Lordships most obliged & obedient
humble servant
THO. GAINSBOROUGH

Bath April 8th 1771

My Lord

I can see plainly your Lordships good nature in not taking amiss what I wrote in my last, 'tho 't is not so clear to me but your Lordship has some suspicion that I meant it to spare myself the trouble of painting another Picture of Lady Dartmouth which time & opportunity may convince your Lordship was not the intention, and I here give it under my hand that I will most willingly begin upon a new Canvas. But I only for the present beg your Lordship will give me leave to try an Experiment upon that Picture to prove the amazing Effect of dress—I mean to treat it as a cast off Picture and dress it (contrary I know to Lady Dartmouths taste) in the modern way; the worst consequence that can attend it will be Her Ladyships being angry with me for a time—I am vastly out in my notion of the thing if the Face does not immediately look like; but I must know if Lady Dartmouth Powders or not in common: I only beg to know that, and to have the Picture sent down to me— I promise this, my Lord, that if I boggle a Month by way of Experiment to please myself, it shall not in the least abate my desire of attempting another to please your Lordship when I can be in London for that purpose or Lady Dartmouth comes to Bath.

> I am
> your Lordships
> most obedient humble
> servant
>
> THO. GAINSBOROUGH

Bath
April 13th 1771

My Lord I am very well aware of the Objection to modern dresses in Pictures, that they are soon out of fashion & look awkward; but as that misfortune cannot be helpd we must set it against the un-luckiness of fancied dresses taking away Likenesses, the principal beauty and intention of a Portrait

18. TO THE EARL OF DARTMOUTH

Here it is then—nothing can be more absurd than the foolish custom of painters dressing people like Scaramouches, and expecting the likeness to appear. Had a picture voice, action, etc. to make itself known as Actors have upon the Stage, no disguise would be

From the Catalogue of the Loan Exhibition in the Birmingham
Museum and Art Gallery, 1902, No. 17
1 The wife of Dr. Philip Ditcher a Bath Surgeon who died in 1781.
She was a daughter of Samuel Richardson. The picture was begun
at Bath before 1774 and finished in 1779, *see E.K.W.* 196

sufficient to conceal a person; but only a face confined to one view and not a muscle to move to say, "Here I am" falls very hard upon the poor Painter who perhaps is not within a mile of the truth in painting the Face only. Your Lordship I'm sure, will be sensible of the effect of the dress thus far, but I defy any but a Painter of some sagacity (and such you see I am, my Lord) to be well aware of the different Effects which one part of a picture has upon another, and how the Eye may be cheated as to the appearance of size, and by an artful management of the accompanyments. A Tune may be so confused by a false Bass—that is if it is ever so plain, simple and full of meaning, it shall become a jumble of nonsense, and just so shall a handsome face be overset by a fictitious bundle of trumpery of the foolish Painter's own inventing. For my part (however your Lordship may suspect my Genius for Lying) I have that regard for truth, that I hold the finest invention as a mere slave in Comparison, and believe I shall remain an ignorant fellow to the end of my days, because I never could have patience to read Poetical impossibilities, the very food of a Painter; especially if he intends to be KNIGHTED in this land of Roast Beef, so well do serious people love froth. But, where am I, my Lord? this my free Opinion in another Line with a witness—forgive me my Lord, I'm but a wild goose at best—all I mean is this, Lady Dartmouth's Picture will look more like and not so large when dressed properly; and if it does not, I'll begin another.

[*April 18th*]

19. TO MRS. DITCHER,[1] LANSDOWN ROAD, BATH

Madam—I am very glad the picture arrived safe and meets with your approbation. With regard to the price of the picture and frame I must acknowledge myself overpaid abundantly by my worthy friend's attention to my family while we lived at Bath, and which I shall ever remember with gratitude. If you can, pardon my neglect in not paying the carriage, which I fully intended doing but for the hurry I was in the day it went away. You must rest assured, Madam, that what remains unpaid is from us to you. My family join in best respects. And I remain, your most obedient servant,

THO. GAINSBOROUGH

Bath, July 31st 1779

54

From the *Ninth Report of the Royal Commission on MS.*, *p.* 481

1 Dr. William Dodd (1729–77) was tutor to the Fifth Earl of Chester-
field, and was convicted for forging his pupil's signature and sentenced
to death

The portrait was painted in 1773, *see E.K.W.* 198

20. TO DR. WILLIAM DODD[1]

Dear Sir,

My wife not being well enough to answer Mrs. Dodd's obliging letter just now, & to acknowledge the receipt & return her most grateful thanks for the kind present, has employed me to do my best, although I confess myself very unequal to the task. If grateful feelings could but make their appearance upon paper with a little drawing instead of writing I should be more likely to express myself clearly upon this subject, for Sir, I can't say my tints in this way are quite so regularly laid upon my pallet as I could wish for Mr. Dodd's inspection. However, it is some comfort to recollect that my worthy friend had heard me talk wild enough in a warm fit not to be frightened at any flight that may dash upon paper. Mrs. Dodd, who has beauty & charms to do justice to any painted silk that ever was touched by the finest pencil, forgets that there is no one here fit for such an elegant dress, but yet her seeming to think them so is a compliment equal to the charm of her generous present.

Such politeness cannot be soon or easily forgotten, & if I was not afraid of taking from the partiality Mrs. Dodd has for your picture as it is now, & I thought it possible to make it ten times handsomer, I would give it a few touches in the warmth of my gratitude, though the ladies say that it is very handsome as it is; for I peep & listen through the keyhole of the door of the painting room on purpose to see how you touch them out of the pulpit as well as in it. Lord! says one, what a lively eye that gentleman has!

We are going this evening to the benefit of a certain musical gentleman who talks of talking by notes ere long, & then I suppose some extempore gentleman will preach by notes. We had a stranger that gave us a strange sermon last Sunday at our chapel, by which I fear our good friend is not well at Weston, but I shall take a walk to see him tomorrow. I have not neglected the chapel one day, *since I took a liking to it*, nor don't mean ever to quit it.

My wife & daughters beg to join in best compliments to Mrs. Dodd & yourself, & I am most truly, Dear Sir,

Your most obliged & humble servant

THO. GAINSBOROUGH

Bath, November 24th, 1773

56

Plate 6

Plate 7
CORNARD WOOD
National Gallery

58

Taken from *Whitley p.* 58

1 Dodsley, James (1724–97) bookseller, brother of John Dodsley the poet dramatist and bookseller, he was himself a writer and a member of the *Congeries* a well-known booksellers' club. He was the London publisher of the *New Bath Guide* by Christopher Anstey, 1766

Taken from *Whitley p.* 208. Sold Sotheby 24th June, 1924, 295(2)

1 Mrs. Dupont, Gainsborough's sister and mother of Gainsborough Dupont who was apprenticed to his uncle in 1772, *see E.K.W. p.* 41

2 John Gainsborough (1711–85) the painter's brother known as *Scheming Jack* because of his passion for designing curiosities such as a cradle which rocked by itself and a cuckoo that sang all the year round. *See Whitley p.* 208 and *Fulcher p.* 16, *et. seq.* For portraits of him *see E.K.W.* 275, *et. seq.*

21. TO JAS. DODSLEY,[1] Pall Mall, London

Sir,—I beg you to accept my sincerest thanks for the favour you have done me concerning the paper for drawings. I had set my heart upon getting some of it, as it is, so completely what I have long been in search of. The mischief of that you were so kind as to enclose is not only the small wires but a large cross wire. . . . which the other has none of, nor hardly any impression of the smallest wire. I wish, Sir, that one of my landskips, such as I could make you upon that paper, would prove a sufficient inducement for you to make still further inquiry. I should think my time well bestowed, however little the value you might with reason set upon it.—I am Sir, your much obliged and most obedient humble servant,

THO. GAINSBOROUGH

Bath, 26th November, 1767

P.S.—I am at this moment viewing the difference of that you sent and the Bath guide, holding them edgeways to the light, and could cry my eyes out to see those furrows. Upon my honour I would give a guinea a quire for a dozen quire of it.

22. TO MRS. DUPONT[1]

I promised John,[2] when he did me the honour of a visit in Town, to allow him half a crown a week, which with what his good cousin Gainsboro' allows him, and sister Gibbon, I hope will (if applied properly *to his own use*) render the remainder of his old age tolerably comfortable, for villainously old he is indeed grown. I have herewith sent you three guineas, with which I beg the favour of you to supply him for half a year with 2s. 6d. per week; paying him what day of the week you judge most good. I should think not on the same days that either sister Gibbon's two shillings is paid, not on those days which his cousin do for him. And that he may not know but what you advance the money out of your own pocket, I have enclosed a letter that you may show him, which may give you a better power to manage him if troublesome to you.

September 29, 1783

Extract of a letter taken from *Whitley p.* 209

1 This and the following letter are taken from *Fulcher pp.* 50 *and* 51. In a footnote (*p.* 50) *Fulcher* says "The address of this letter has been destroyed; and all that remains of the superscription of the next one is 'ey at Law, in Colchester'. They were probably inscribed to his friend, Mr. Robert Edgar, who, at that time practised there as a lawyer." Gainsborough painted various members of the Edgar family, *see* *E.K.W.* 231–234

I beg the favour of you to advance half a crown a week to Brother John, for his own use, from this Michaelmas, and I will pay you again the first opportunity. I thought what I gave him when in London sufficient to last till this time, which is the reason I did not trouble you with a line sooner.

24. TO A CLIENT IN COLCHESTER PROBABLY MR. ROBERT EDGAR[1]

Sir,

I am favored with your obliging letter, and shall finish your picture in two or three days at farthest, and send to Colchester according to your order, with a frame. I thank you, Sir, for your kind intention of procuring me a few Heads to paint when I come over, which I purpose doing as soon as some of those are finished which I have in hand. I should be glad [if] you'd place your picture as far from the light as possible; observing to let the light fall from the left. Favor me with a faithful account of what is generally thought of it; and as to my bill, it will be time enough when I see you,

Who am, Sir,

Your most obed[t] hum[e] serv[t],

THO. GAINSBOROUGH

Ipswich, Feb. 24th. 1757

25. MR. ROBERT EDGAR

Sir,

I am favor'd with your obliging letter, and return you many thanks for your kind intention; I thought I should have been at Colchester by this time, as I promis'd my sister I would the first opportunity, but business comes in and being chiefly in the Face way, I'm afraid to put people off when they are in the mind to sit. You please me much by saying that no other fault is found in your picture than the roughness of the surface, for that part being of use in giving force to the effect at a proper distance, and what a judge of painting knows an original from a copy by; in short being the touch of the pencil, which is harder to preserve than smoothness. I am much better pleas'd that they should spy out things of that kind, than to see an eye half an inch out of its place, or a nose out of drawing when viewed at a proper distance. I don't think it would be more

1 Probably John Clubbe, rector of Wheatfield, the author of a Tract (first published in 1758) intended as a satire on conjectural Etymologists, entitled *The History and Antiquities of the ancient Villa of Wheatfield*

This and the previous letter are an interesting comment on Gainsborough's technique, *see Introduction p.* 16

From *Whitley*, unpublished papers, British Museum; sold Puttick and Simpson, 3 June, 1921, together with a portrait

1 What appears to be the first portrait of Garrick by Gainsborough was exhibited at the Society of Artists, Spring Gardens in April 1766, No. 50. It was adversely criticised by the *Public Advertiser*, *see Whitley p.* 45. In the portrait Garrick had his arm around a bust of Shakespeare. This is probably the picture which Gainsborough remodelled for the Stratford Commission and delivered in 1769 and which was burnt in 1946, *see* the two following letters

ridiculous for a person to put his nose close to the canvas and say the
colours smell offensive, than to say how rough the paint lies; for
one is just as material as the other with regard to hurting the effect
and drawing of a picture. Sir Godfrey Kneller used to tell them that
pictures were not made to smell of: and what made his pictures more
valuable than others with the connoisseurs was his pencil or touch.
I hope, Sir you'll pardon this dissertation upon pencil and touch,
for if I gain no better point than to make you and Mr. Clubb[1] laugh
when you next meet at the sign of the Tankard, I shall be very well
contented. I'm sure I could not paint his picture for laughing he gave
such a description of eating and drinking at that place. I little
thought you were a Lawyer when I said, not one in ten was worth
hanging. I told Clubb, of that, and he seemed [to] think I was
lucky that I did not say one in a hundred. It's too late to ask your
pardon now, but really Sir, I never saw one of your profession look
so honest in my life, and that's the reason I concluded you were in
the wool trade. Sir Jaspar Wood was so kind [as] to set me right,
otherwise perhaps I should have made more blunders.

I am,

Sir, your most obed^t & obliged hum. serv^{t.}

THO. GAINSBOROUGH

Ipswich, Mar. 13th 1758

26. TO DAVID GARRICK

Dont think that I am in the least angry with any of our friends at
the Exhibition[1] I dont look upon it as it is conducted at present to be
calculated so much to bring out good painters as bad ones. There is
certainly a false taste & an impudent style prevailing which if
Vandyke was living would put him out of countenance; and I think
even his work would appear so opposed to such a glare. Nature is
modest and the artist should be so in his addresses to Her.

[*Bath 1766*]

Plate 8
THE DUKE OF BEDFORD
Trinity College, Dublin

Plate 9
TWO SHEPHERD BOYS WITH DOGS FIGHTING
Iveagh Bequest Kenwood

F

From the original in the Forster Collection of Garrick Correspondence, Vol. X, in the Victoria and Albert Museum

1 Derrick, the Master of Ceremonies at Bath
2 The portraits are in the collection of the Duke of Buccleuch at Bowhill, *see E.K.W.* 490–491
3 *The Watering Place* (*Pl.* 14) now in the National Gallery, London
The letter is endorsed on the back in Garrick's hand. *A letter from Gainsborough about Shakespeare and my picture 1768.* It was probably written in the summer of 1768 and some weeks before the next letter. Gainsborough was either working on another version of the portrait of 1766, or remodelling it as he was dissatisfied with the first version. It was clearly not intended at that time for the Jubilee celebrations at Stratford as Gainsborough first heard of this in December 1768

From the original in the Forster Collection of Garrick Correspondence, Vol. X, in the Victoria and Albert Museum

Dear Sir, I take particular notice of your friendly Anxiety for my 67
recovery. I do assure you, and thank you most kindly for your *sharp*
thought but having had 12 oz: of Blood taken immediately away am
perfectly recovered, strong in the Back and *able* so make your
sublime self easy—I suppose your Letter to Mr. Sharp was upon no
other Business, so have inclosed it—But observe, I thank you sincerely.

Shakespeare shall come forth forthwith as the Lawyer says—
damn the Original Picture of him *with your leave*, for I think a
stupider Face I never beheld except D—k's.[1]

I intend, with your approbation, my dear Friend, to take the
form from his Pictures & statues just enough to preserve his likeness
past the doubt of all blockheads, at first sight, and supply a *soul* from his
Works—it is impossible that such a Mind and Ray of Heaven
could shine, with such a Face and pair of Eyes as that Picture has;
so as I said before, damn *that*.

I'm going to dinner, and after, I'll try a sketch—I shall leave
the *Price* to you—I don't care whether I have a farthing if you will
but let me do it—to be sure I should never ask more than my
Portrait price (which is 60 guineas), but perhaps ought to ask less,
as there is no confinement of Painting from Life but I say I leave it to
you, promising to be contented *upon Honor*. I could wish you to
call *upon any pretence* any day after next Wednesday at the Duke of
Montagu, because you'd see the Duke and Duchess in my *last*
manner;[2] but not as if you thought anything of mine worth that
trouble, only to see his Grace's Landskip of Rubens,[3] and the 4
Vandykes whole length in his Grace's dressing-room.

[*1768*]

Dear Sir,

I doubt I stand accused (if not accursed) all this time of my
neglect for not going to Stratford, and giving you a Line from thence
as I promised; but, Lord, what can one do such Weather as this,
continual Rains; My Genius is so dampt by it that I can do nothing
to please me. I have been several days rubbing in & rubbing out
my design for Shakespeare and damme if I think I shall let it go or
let you see it at last—I was willing like an Ass as I am, to expose
myself a little out of the simple Portrait way, and had a notion of

1 Almost certainly the bust by an unknown artist now in the Parish Church at Stratford-on-Avon

2 Hannah Pritchard (1711–68) actress who appeared at the principal London theatres and was considered the best Lady Macbeth of her day

1 This is a copy of the receipt sent to the Corporation of Stratford-on-Avon, and is taken from a scrap-book composed by George Daniel Islington (1759–64) entitled *Stratford Jubilee Volume*, which is in the British Museum. There is in the Chamberlain's accounts at Stratford-on-Avon for 1769, an item: To Mr. Gainsborough for Mr. Garrick's picture £63. 0. 0.

The Stratford festival in honour of Shakespeare was held in the Autumn of 1769. A new town hall had been built and the Corporation appealed to Garrick in a letter dated 6th December, 1768, to present a statue, bust or portrait of Shakespeare and if possible one of himself. It seems likely that the picture in Stratford town hall, until the fire in 1946, was the original of 1766 possibly remodelled for the commission, since no other full length version of the picture is known, and from the evidence of the two previous letters Gainsborough was clearly working on the subject, *see Whitley p.* 67

showing where that inimitable Poet had his Ideas from, by an immediate Ray darting down upon his Eye turn'd up for the purpose; but G— damn it I can make nothing of my Ideas there has been such a fall of rain from the same quarter—you shall not see it for I'll cut it out before you can come—tell me Dear Sir when you purpose coming to Bath, that I may be quick enough in my Motions. Shakespeare's Bust[1] is a silly smiling thing, and I have not sense enough to make him more sensible in the Picture and so I tell ye you shan't see it. I must make a plain Picture of Him standing erect, and give it an old look as if it had been Painted at the time he lived and there we shall fling 'em Damme.

Poor Mrs. Pritchard[2] died here on Saturday night 11 o'clock—so now her performance being no longer present to those who must see and hear, before they can believe, will you know my dear sir—but I beg pardon, I forgot—Time puts us all into his Fobb, as I do my Timekeeper, *watch* that my dear.

Who am I but the same

Think you

T.G.

"Impudent scroundrel says Mr. G.—Blackguard."

Bath 22nd Ag[st]. 1768

29. RECEIPT FOR THE PORTRAIT OF DAVID GARRICK, FORMERLY AT STRATFORD ON AVON[1]

recd of the Corporation of Stratford upon Avon, by the hands of David Garrick, Esq. sixty-three pounds & in full for a whole length portrait of that Gentleman.

£63.

THOMAS GAINSBOROUGH

Extracts from Sotheby's Catalogue 28th June, 1927 (395)

1 This probably refers to the gift of a drawing – Gainsborough often made presents of his sketches to his friends

From *The Private Correspondence of David Garrick*, published by Harry Colburn and Richard Bentley, 1831

... with this sensible skull of mine I have order'd my Business so as to have three sitters one after another to-morrow, besides having caught a d—m'd cold by riding in the rain this afternoon, so that I cannot call ... to take my leave of you to-morrow ... I shall never think any touch of my hand capable of expressing a hundredth part of my obligation and gratitude to you and that if I ever spy but a glimmering of any acknowledgment for the Chalk scratch[1] ... except you speaking kindly of me I swear by Saint Luke's pencil you shall never see touch, scratch or blot more of

My Dear Friend

Yours very sincerely,

THO. GAINSBOROUGH

Tuesday evening [*No date*]

31. TO DAVID GARRICK

Dear Sir,

I, as well as the rest of the world, acknowledge your riches, and know your princely spirit; but all will not do, for, as I told you before, I am already overpaid for the shabby performance; and if you have a mind to make me happier than all the presents London can afford, you must do it by never thinking yourself at all in my debt. I wished many years for the happiness of Mr. Garrick's acquaintance, and pray, dear Sir, let me now enjoy it quietly; for sincerely and truly I shall not be easy if you give way to any of your romantic whimsies, & besides, d—n it, I thought you knew me too well, you who can read hearts and faces both at a view, and that at first sight too. Come, if you will not plague me any more upon this frightful subject, I will tell you a story about *first sight.* You must know, Sir, whilst I lived at Ipswich, there was a benefit concert in which a new song was to be interduced, and I being Steward, went to the honest cabinet-maker who was our singer instead of a better, and asked him if he could sing at sight, for that I had a new song with all the parts wrote out. "Yes, Sir" said he "I can". Upon which I order Mr. Giardini of Ipswich to begin the Symphony, & gave my signal for the attention of the company; but behold, a dead silence followed the Symphony instead of the song; upon which I jumped up to the fellow: "D—n you, why dont you sing? did not you tell

1 Isaac Gossett (1713–99) invented a composition of wax in which he modelled portraits which brought him much patronage including that of members of the royal family. Gainsborough was himself an amateur at wax modelling and painted a portrait of Gossett, *see E.K.W.* 320

From the original in the Forster Collection of Garrick Correspondence, Vol. X, in the Victoria and Albert Museum

The editor of *The Private Correspondence of David Garrick*, see above, notes "this is the front view of Garrick, in laced clothes with a book in the right hand. It is more genteel than Sir Joshua's – I mean that great painter's front view of him. Gainsborough's though extremely like, gives what is a common fault, the impression of a larger figure than that of the sitter. How either painter could be reconciled to the abominable *wigs* of the time, saddling the forehead in the most expressive part of it, they have not condescended to inform us." There appear to be three versions of this picture: one for Mrs. Garrick, one for James Clutterbuck, and one for Dr. Schomberg, *see E.K.W.* 305–307

From the original in the Forster Collection of Garrick Correspondence, Vol. X, in the Victoria and Albert Museum

1 James Clutterbuck of Bath, Garrick's friend and business adviser

me you could sing at first *sight?*". "Yes, please your honour, I did say I could sing at sight, but not *first* sight."

I am, dear Sir, your most obedient humble servant.

Bath July 27, 1768

P.S. I beg, Sir, you will leave the affair of Gossett[1] to me. I shall give him a bill payable at first sight, I assure you.

32. TO DAVID GARRICK

Dear Sir,

I ask pardon for having kept your Picture so long from Mrs. Garrick. It has indeed been of great service in keeping me going, but my chief reason for detaining it so long was the hopes of getting one copy *like*, to hang in my own Parlour, not as a show Picture, but for my own enjoyment, to look when I please at a Great Man, who has thought me worthy of some little notice; but not one copy can I make which does not as much resemble Mr. Garrick's Brother as Himself—so I have bestow'd a drop of excellent Varnish to keep you out, instead of a falling tear at parting, and have only to beg of Dear Mrs. Garrick to hang it in the best light she can find out, and to continue puffing for me in the manner Mr. Keate informs me she does. That you may long continue to delight & suprize the World with your *Original* Face whilst I hobble after with my Copy

Is the sincere wish

of Dear Sir

your most unaccountable

& obediant servant

THO. GAINSBOROUGH

Bath. June 22nd 1772

P.S.–The picture is to go to London by Wiltshire's flying waggon on Wednesday next; and I believe will arrive by Saturday morning.

33. TO DAVID GARRICK

My Dear Sir,

I never will consent that anybody makes a present of your Face to Clutterbuck[1] but myself, because I always intended a Copy (*by my own hand*) for Him, that he may one day tell me what to do with my Money, the only thing he understands except jeering of folks.

2 Probably refers to a gift of drawing

From the original in the Yale University Library
The *Middlesex Journal* commenting upon Gainsborough's pictures shown at the Royal Academy in 1772 remarks "his colours are too glowing. It would be well for him if he would borrow a little of the modest colouring of Sir Joshua Reynolds". It may be that Gainsborough was piqued by this criticism, *see Whitley p.* 87
A copy of this letter, not in Gainsborough's hand, is in the Forster collection of Garrick Correspondence, in the Victoria and Albert Museum, and is headed, *Gainsborough to Mr. Garrick Bath Sunday Morning, 1772*

I shall look upon it that you break in upon my Line of happiness in this World if you mention it; and for the Original, it was to be my present to Mrs. Garrick, and so it shall be in spite of your blood—Now for the Chalk scratch[2] it's a poor affair, not much like the young Ladies, but however if you don't remember what I said in my last, and caution your Brother of the same *Rock*, may you sink in the midst of your Glory.

I know your great stomach and that you hate to be cram'd, but by G— you shall swallow this one bait, and when you speak of me don't let it be like a Goose but remember you are a fat Turkey.

God bless all your endeavours to delight the World, and may you sparkle to the last.—

THO. GAINSBOROUGH

damn Underwood

34. TO DAVID GARRICK

My dear Sir,

When the streets are paved with Brilliants, and the Skies made of Rainbows I suppose you'l be contented, and satisfied with Red blue & yellow—It appears to me that Fashion, let it consist of false or true taste will have its run, like a runaway Horse; for when Eyes & Ears are thoroughly debauch'd by Glare & Noise, the returning to modest truth will seem very gloomy for a time; and I know you are cursedly puzzled how to make this retreat without putting out your lights, and losing the advantage of all our new discoveries of transparent Painting etc, etc. How to satisfye your tawdry Friends, whilst you steal back into the mild Evening gleam and quiet middle time.

Now I'll tell you my sprightly Genius how this is to be done—maintain all your Light, but spare the poor abused Colors, til the Eye rests and recovers—Keep up your Music by supplying the place of *Noise* by more Sound, more Harmony & more Tune, and split that curs'd Fife & Drum.

Whatever so great a Genius as Mr. Garrick may say or do to support our false taste, He must feel the truth of what I am now saying, that neither our Plays, Painting or Music are any longer real works of Invention but the abuse of Nature's lights and [what] has already been invented in [former] times.

Adieu my dear Friend

Any Comm^ds to Bath

Taken from *Fulcher p.* 105

1 Mrs. Gibbon. Gainsborough's sister Sarah, who let apartments in Bath
2 His brother Humphrey like John had a faculty for mechanics and engineering, but was more practical than his brother. He was awarded a premium by the Society of Arts for a drill-plough and a tide mill and he seems to have superintended the making of some new roads near Henley where he was the Methodist Minister. He is also said to have invented the method of condensing steam in a separate vessel, which was of great service to James Watt. Thicknesse in his Memoir of the painter says that Gainsborough gave him Humphrey's model of a steam engine when he died in 1776, *see Fulcher p.* 19

Sunday Morning.

A Word to the Wise; if you let your Portrait hang up so high, only to consult your Room, and to insinnuate something over the other Door, it never can look without a hardness of Countenance and the Painting flat, it was calculated for breast high and will never have its Effect or likeness otherwise.

35. TO MRS. GIBBON[1]

Dear Sister,

We return you our best thanks for the excellent present of fish, which turned out as good as ever was eaten, and came very timely for brother Humphry[2] to take part with us. He went home to Henley to-day, having been with us ten days, which was as long as he could well be absent from his business of collecting the tolls upon the river. He was as well as could be expected, considering his affliction for the loss of his poor wife. We did all we could to comfort him, and wish him every possible happiness, as he is a good creature. My wife has been but very indifferent with the disorder that goes about in all parts of London; it seems to be a sort of cold attended with a bad cough, and it has gone through our family, servants and all; but, thank God, we are upon the mending hand: we don't hear of many people dying of it, though 'tis universal. I am glad to hear business in the lodging-house way goes on so well. I know you would willingly keep the cart upon the wheels, till you go to heaven, though you deserve to ride there in something better. I told Humphry you were a rank Methodist, who says you had better be a Presbyterian, but I say Church of England. It does not signify what, if you are but free from hypocrisy, and don't set your heart upon worldly honors and wealth. I wish you long life and happiness, and remain,

Your affectionate brother,

THO. GAINSBOROUGH

London, Nov. 13th 1775

Taken from *Whitley p.* 121

1 Gainsborough's younger daughter Margaret (1752–1820)

2 Gainsborough's elder daughter Mary (1748–1826)

3 Fischer, Johann Christian (1733–1800). Oboist and composer; settled in London in 1768 and in 1780 became Musician to Queen Charlotte. Noted for his solo oboe playing which was a feature of the London concerts organised by J. C. Bach and Abel. Mozart immortalised a Minuet by Fischer by writing variations on it (K.179). Gainsborough's elder daughter Mary married Fischer in February 1780 without asking her father's advice, it was an unhappy marriage which soon came to an end. Gainsborough's portrait of his son-in-law is now in the possession of H.M. the Queen at Buckingham Palace, *see E.K.W.* 252

4 Mrs. Dupont

Dear Sister,—I received yours and am glad your Houses and every thing go on so much to your satisfaction. I have always wish'd you happy, though sometimes we have differ'd a little in our opinions. I did all in my power to comfort poor Humphry, and should have been glad of his company a little longer, had not his business called him thence.

What will become of me time must show; I can only say that my present situation with regard to encouragement is all that heart can wish, but as all wordly success is precarious I don't build happiness, or the expectation of it, upon present appearances. I have built upon sandy foundations all my life long. All I know is that I live at a full thousand pounds a year expense, and will work hard and do my best to go through withal; and if that will not do let those take their lot of blame and sufferings that fall short of their duty, both towards me and themselves. Had I been blessed with your penetration and blind eye towards fool's pleasures, I had steer'd my course better, but we are born with different Passions and gifts, and I have only to hope that the Great Giver of All will make better allowance for us than we can make for one another.

I could now enter into particulars as my heart finds itself affected but what would it all signify? If I tell you my wife is weak but good, and never much formed to humour my Happiness, what can you do to alter her? If I complain that Peggy[1] is a sensible good Girl, but Insolent and proud in her behaviour to me at times, can you make your arm long enough to box her ears for me whilst you live at Bath? And (what has hurt me most of late) were I to unfold a secret and tell you that I have detected a sly trick in Molly[2] by a sight I got of one of her Letters, forsooth, to Mr. Fischer,[3] what could all your cleverness do for me there? and yet I wish for your Head-piece to catch a little more of the secret, for I don't choose to be flung under the pretence of Friendship. I have never suffered that worthy Gentleman ever to be in their Company since I came to London; and behold while I had my eye upon Peggy, the other Slyboots, I suppose, has all along been the Object. Oh, d—n him, he must take care how he trips me off the foot of all happiness.

I desire, my Dear Sister, you will not impart a syllable of what you have here, and believe me ever yours most affectionately,

THOS. GAINSBOROUGH

December 26, 1775

Compliments of this happy season to you and love to Sally.[4]

P.S.—She does not suspect I saw the letter.

80

Dear Sir

I must beg pardon for not answering your Letter sooner, I have had some
plaguesome Sitters, and a sick House besides,
but thank God all is right again. Molly had
a smart Fever at the time I rec'd your Letter,
but My next door neighbour Doctor Heberden
sent Her to Chiswick for Air, and now she is
purely as my Friend Bob said to the old woman.

I hope all your fears and apprehensions about
Him are only signs of your feeling quicker and
deeper than the generality of Parents, which you
certainly do, and that His complaint is by
this time removed. I'll trust you for taking Him

under your Eye the moment He ailes anything
and I think you right, for a stitch in time
spares nine says Bobby's Old Woman —

By dear Doctor I forgot entirely
that you had a Copy of the little Dutch Spirit
of my Blood, 'tis not worth a Farthing, so do
what you please with it, hang it in your ship
as a Scarecrow where it may not be compared
with the Original, and I shall be easy; I
give it to Mother Gibbon but she delights
not in Worldly Prospects, I have a d—nd
plague with Her when she comes to Town, to
find out new Methodist Chapels enough for
Her, for she Prays double Tides, and cares not

a farthing for what Bishop can say, 'tis that same old
Devil that will work a chitmy [chimney] perfume by them

Pray my best respects to your
Family & am Dear Sir

Your ever Faithful & obd't
Serv't
Rich'd Jones Langford

Postscript
4th Jan'y 1779

Tell Bob he will certainly find a cure for his Son in
the French natural History of Bristol Hot Wells &c.

Plate 11

81

THE COUNTESS OF DARTMOUTH
The Earl of Dartmouth

82

37. TO MRS. MARY GIBBON, MILLINER, ABBY CHURCHYARD, BATH

[Word "Circus" appears below address]

Dear Sister,

I rec'd your Letter and am glad to learn everything go to your satisfaction, and Rejoyce in my Heart that you are in that way which is sure to end in peace and eternal happiness—I would have everybody enjoy, unmolested, their own opinions tho I have sometimes said things to try the Temper, but I doubt not your good sense could see, and pardon.

For my Part I despair not, as I am conscious of having done my utmost, tho against all rebuffs and discouragements possible from Ignorance and evil spirits, and at the last hazard and tryal of my own Constitution, with this reward, that *I stand now just where I did;* whereas if I had had my own way (with all my mighty Vices) I should have wasted many thousands—My present situation is that of being as much encouraged as the World can bestow, with every success in my business, but in the other scale, counteracted with disobedience Pride and insolence, and eternal obraidings & reflections—I was induced to try how far Jealousy might be cured by giving into her Hands every Farthing of the Money as I earned it, but very soon found that (as a punishment for so unmanly a condescention) instead of convincing, it was a further incouragment to Govern me, and invert the order of Nature in making the Head the foot and the foot the Head; so that now I have taken the staff into my own hands again, and purpose (God willing) to try my own Virtue and strength to walk straight and do the best for my Children let them follow the Vanity of the Age, or weakness of their leader as they will—I am at an Age now to see right from wrong; and have a pretty good knowledge of Mankind—and I trust if I do my best, all will be well through the merits of Him who hath promised to make good our failings if we trust sincerely—I thank God we are all pretty well except my own Health which has been but indifferent of late. Bro: Humphrey was here lately, and is as happy as could be expected—I leave you to act as you see proper in the affair of Penny's Money, it may be of use to me when you can get it, and you'l be so good as to remit it.

Believe me ever yours most

affectionatly,

THO. GAINSBOROUGH

84

From *Fulcher p.* 107
1 *See* note on *p.* 76

From *Fulcher p.* 108
1 Afterward Mrs. William Villebois, *see E.K.W.* 696. For the Read family, *see* Collins Baker, *Catalogue of British Painting in the Huntington Collection*, 1936, *p.* 49
2 Sam Kilderbee was Town Clerk of Ipswich, when Gainsborough lived there he was Mrs. Gainsborough's legal adviser, after her husband's death

From *Fulcher p.* 118

38. TO MRS. GIBBON

Dear Sister,

I have been going to write to you every post for this month past, but was desirous of acquainting you with what I had done towards settling my brother Humphry's affairs, and therefore postponed writing till I had sold the stock. . . . Mr. Cooper advises me to keep on the house till we can make the most of the steam-engine,[1] (as the work, if taken to pieces, perhaps may never be put together again,) and also the maid in the house, lest any discovery should be made of it. The goods are sold, but none of the books, nor have I had any account yet from Henley, so as to be able to settle anything. We hope you and Sally continue in good health and good bustling spirits, and join in best affections to you both,

T.G.

Nov 5th 1776

39. EXTRACT FROM A LETTER TO MRS. GIBBON

Miss Read,[1] Sir Benjamin Truman's grand-daughter coming out of Wiltshire on purpose to sit. . . . My family had a great desire to make a journey to Ipswich to Mr. and Mrs. Kilderbee[2] for a fortnight and last Sunday morning I packed them off in their own coach with David on horseback; and Molly wrote to me to let me know that they had arrived very safe— but somehow or other they seem desirous of returning rather sooner than the proposed time, as they desire me to go for them by next Tuesday; the bargin was that I should fetch them home. I don't know what's the matter, either people don't pay them honour enough for ladies that *keep a coach*, or else Madam is afraid to trust me alone in this great town.

[*Autumn 1777*]

40. TO MRS. GIBBON

Dear Sister,— I imagine you are by this time no stranger to the alteration which has taken place in my family. The notice I had of it was very sudden, as I had not the least suspicion of the attachment being so long and deeply settled; and as it was too late for me to alter anything, without being the cause of total unhappiness on both sides, my *consent*, which was a mere compliment to affect to ask, I

Taken from Sotheby's Catalogue 24th June, 1924, 295(4)
1 Elizabeth, Gainsborough's youngest sister, later Mrs. Bird settled in
Sudbury

From the original letter in the British Museum, probably about 1764
1 Gainsborough is referring to the topographical views of Paul Sandby
(1725–1809) and comparing them with the ideal landscapes of Gaspar
Poussin and Claude. His own inclination was for *compositions in the
landscape way*, *see* letter to Jackson *p.* 99 and Introduction *p.* 19

needs must give, whether such a match was agreeable to me or not, I would not have the cause of unhappiness lay upon my conscience; and accordingly they were married last Monday, and are settled for the present in a ready furnished little house in Curzon Street, Mayfair. I can't say I have any reason to doubt the man's honesty or goodness of heart, as I never heard anyone speak anything amiss of him; and as to his oddities and temper, she must learn to like as she likes his person, for nothing can be altered now. I pray God she may be happy with him and have her health. Peggy has been very unhappy about it, but I endeavour to comfort her, in hope that she will have more pride and goodness than to do anything without first asking my advice and approbation. We shall see how they go on, and I shall write to you further upon the subject. I hope you are all well, and with best wishes,—I remain your affectionate Bro.

THOS. GAINSBOROUGH

Feb 23rd 1780

41. TO MRS. GIBBON

My Dear Sister,

I was extremely sorry to find by your last Letter, that you could suppose me offended in the least degree by what you said in your former; I hope My dear we have more affection for each other, if not more sense, than to suffer what may be said in Joke to make any material difference in our good wishes towards each other; I assure you what I said was without the least intention of offending, I only meant *in my own manner* to urge all parties to claim their Right; and to set all Joking aside, I do think that Poor Betsey[1] should be allowed something besides her share in other respects to reward her giving up what she might so reasonably expect to recover by Law—I meant no

. . . . . .

July 31. 1787

42. TO LORD HARDWICKE

Mr. Gainsborough presents his Humble respects to Lord Hardwicke; and shall always think it an honor to be employ'd in anything for his Lordship; but with respect to *real Views* from Nature in this Country he has never seen any Place that affords a Subject equal to the poorest imitations of Gaspar or Claude. Paul Sanby[1] is the only

Plate 12
THE COUNTESS OF DARTMOUTH
The Earl of Dartmouth

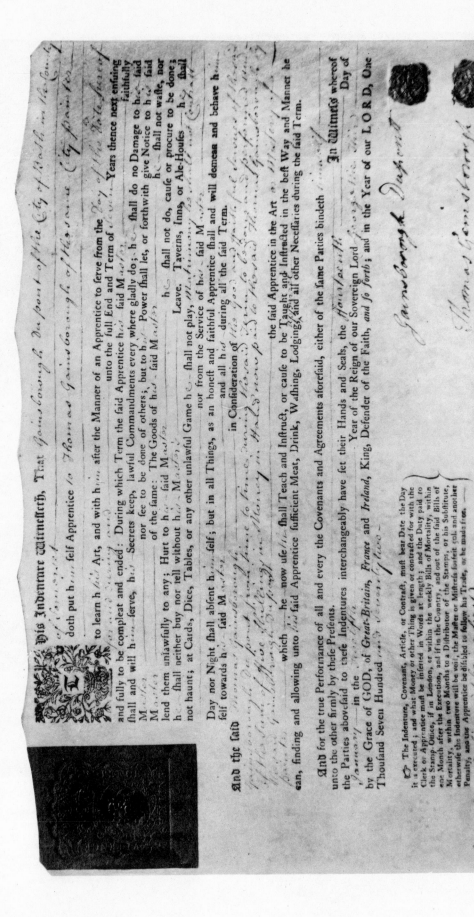

This Indenture Witnesseth, That *Gainsborough Dupont of the City of Bath in the County of Somerset* doth put *himself* Apprentice to *Thomas Gainsborough of the same City, painter* ____ to learn *his* Art, and with *him* after the Manner of an Apprentice to serve from the Day of the Date hereof ____ unto the full End and Term of *seven* Years thence next ensuing ____ and fully to be compleat and ended: During which Term the said Apprentice *his* said *Master* faithfully shall and will *him* serve, *his* Secrets keep, *his* lawful Commandments every where gladly do; *he* shall do no Damage to *his* said *Master* ____ nor see to be done of others; but to *his* Power shall let, or forthwith give Notice to *his* said *Master* ____ of the same: The Goods of *his* said *Master* ____ *he* shall not waste, nor lend them unlawfully to any; Hurt to *his* said *Master* ____ *he* shall not do, cause or procure to be done; *he* shall neither buy nor sell without *his* Master's Leave. Taverns, Inns, or Ale-Houses *he* shall not haunt; at Cards, Dice, Tables, or any other unlawful Game *he* shall not play, *Matrimony he shall not* Con-tract ____ nor from the Service of *his* said *Master* ____ Day nor Night shall absent *himself*; but in all Things, as an honest and faithful Apprentice shall and will demean and behave *him*-self towards *his* said *Master* ____ and all *his* during all the said Term.

And the said *Thomas Gainsborough* ____ *in Consideration of the good and faithful Services of the said Gainsborough Dupont and also in consideration of the sum of one hundred pounds to him paid by the said Gainsborough Dupont* ____ *the receipt of five hundred pounds of lawful Money in Hand received by the said Thomas Gainsborough* ____ *the said Gainsborough Dupont* ____ the said Apprentice in the Art *or Mistery* ____ which *he* now use *which he* shall Teach and Instruct, or cause to be Taught and Instructed in the best Way and Manner he can, finding and allowing unto *the* said Apprentice sufficient Meat, Drink, Washing, Lodging, and all other Necessaries during the said Term.

And for the true Performance of all and every the Covenants and Agreements aforesaid, either of the same Parties bindeth *himself* ____ unto the other firmly by these Presents. **In Witness** whereof the Parties above-said to these Indentures interchangeably have set their Hands and Seals, the *Fourteenth* ____ Day of *January* ____ in the *Twelfth* ____ Year of the Reign of our Sovereign Lord *George the Third* by the Grace of GOD, of *Great-Britain, France* and *Ireland,* King, Defender of the Faith, *and so forth*; and in the Year of our LORD, One Thousand Seven Hundred *and Seventy two.*

☞ The Indenture, Covenant, Article, or Contract, must bear Date the Day it is executed; and what Money or other Thing is given or contracted for with the Clerk or Apprentice must be inserted in Words at length; and the Duty paid to the Stamp-Office, if in London, or within the weekly Bills of Mortality, within one Month after the Execution, and if in the Country, and out of the said Bills of Mortality, within two Months to a Distributor of the Stamps, or his Substitute, otherwise the Indenture will be void, the Master or Mistress forfeit 50l. and another Penalty, and the Apprentice be disabled to follow his Trade, or be made free.

Sealed and Delivered (being first
duly Stampt) in the Presence of
J. Page — Mary Gainsborough

Gainsborough Dupont

Thomas Gainsborough

Plate 13
APPRENTICESHIP INDENTURE BETWEEN THOS. GAINSBOROUGH R.A. AND HIS
NEPHEW GAINSBOROUGH DUPONT. BATH. JANUARY 12TH 1772
Messrs. Frost and Reid

H

From the original letter in the possession of the Courtauld Institute, London University

1 Thomas Harvey (1747–1819) a master weaver in Norwich. During the last quarter of the eighteenth century he formed an important collection of paintings, including examples by Cuyp, Hobbema, Gaspar Poussin, Tintoretto and Wilson. He owned Gainsborough's *Cottage Door* now in the Huntingdon Collection in California, *Pl.* 19

See Francis Hawcroft, *Crome and his Patron Thomas Harvey of Catton, Connoisseur*, December 1959, *pp.* 232–237

Man of Genius, he believes, who has employ'd his Pencil that way—
Mr. G. hopes Lord Hardwicke will not mistake his meaning, but if
his Lordship wishes to have anything tolerable of the name of G,
the subject altogether, as well as figures etc. must be of his own
Brain; otherwise Lord Hardwicke will only pay for Encouraging a
Man out of his way and had much better buy a picture of some of the
good Old Masters.

Saturday Morning

43. TO MR. THOMAS HARVEY[1] AT CATTON NEAR NORWICH

Dear Sir,

Your very obliging Letter inclosing a Norwich Bank Bill, Value
seventy three Pounds, on Messrs Vere & Williams. I acknowledge
when pd to be in full for the Landscape with Cows & all demands.

I am glad Sir, that the Picture got no damage; if ever you should
find anything of a Chill come upon the Varnish of my Pictures,
owing to its being a spirit of wine Vanish, take a rag, or little bit of
sponge, with Nut oil, and rub it til the mist clears away, and
then wipe as much of it off as a few strokes with a clean Cloth—will
Effect this done once or twice a year after damp weather you will
find convenient—My swelled Neck is got very painful indeed, but I
hope is the [?] near coming to a Cure—How happy should I be to
set out for Yarmouth and after recruiting my poor Crazy Frame,
enjoy the coasting along til I reach'd Norwich and give you a call—
God only knows what is for me, but hope is the Pallat Colors we all
paint with in sickness—'tis odd how all the Childish passions hang
about me in sickness, I feel such a fondness for my first imitations of
little Dutch Landskips that I can't keep from working an hour or
two of a Day, though with a great mixture of bodily Pain—I am so
childish that I could make a Kite, catch Gold Finches, or build
little Ships—

Believe me Dear Sir
with the greatest sincerity
your ever Obliged & Obedient
Servant

THO. GAINSBOROUGH

Pall Mall
May 22nd 1788

P.S. I have recollected that a Stamp Red. may be proper.

This letter and the next one are taken from J. Ireland, *The Letters and Poems of J.H. with Anecdotes of his life*, London 1786, *p.* 12. They were printed in the *Public Advertiser*, 20th June, 1786

1 Henderson, John (1747–85) known as the Bath Roscius, appeared in Hamlet at Bath in 1772 under the name of Courtney. Later appeared at Drury Lane and Covent Garden. He also drew, etched and wrote poems and, with Sheridan, published *Practical Method of Reading and Writing English Poetry*

For his portraits by Gainsborough, *see E.K.W.* 360 *and* 361

He clearly did not take Gainsborough's advice, as he was later playing Falstaff.

Dear Henderson,

If you had not written to me as you did, I should have concluded you had been laid down; pray, my boy, take care of yourself this hot weather, and don't run about London streets, fancying you are catching strokes of nature, at the hazard of your constitution. It was my first school, and deeply read in petticoats I am, therefore you may allow me to caution you. Stick to Garrick as close as you can, for your life: you should follow his heels like his shadow in sunshine. No one can be so near him as yourself, when you please; and I'm sure, when he sees it strongly as other people do, he must be fond of such an *ape*. You have nothing to do now but to stick to the few great ones of the earth, who seem to have offered you their assistance in bringing you to light, and to brush off all the low ones as fast as they light upon you. You see I hazard the appearing a puppy in your eyes, but pretending to advise you, from real regard, and the sincere desire I have of seeing you a great and happy man. Garrick is the greatest creature living, in every respect: he is worth studying in every action. Every view, and every idea of him, is worthy of being stored up for imitation; and I have ever found him a generous and a sincere friend. Look upon him Henderson, with your imitative eyes, for when he drops, you'll have nothing but poor old Nature's book to look in. You'll be left to grope about alone, scratching your pate in the dark, or by a farthing candle. Now is your time, my lively fellow! And, do ye hear, don't eat so devilishly; you'll get too fat when you rest from playing, or get a sudden jog by illness to bring you down again.

> Adieu, my dear H.,
> Believe me your's, &c.,
> T.G.

Bath, 27th June, 1773

45. TO JOHN HENDERSON

Dear Henderson,

If one may judge by your last spirited epistle, you are in good keeping; no one eats with a more grateful countenance, or swallows with more good nature than yourself. If this does not seem sense, do but recollect how many hard-featured fellows there are in the world that frown in the midst of enjoyment, chew with unthankfulness, and seem to swallow with pain instead of pleasure; now any one who sees you eat pig and plum-sauce, immediately feels that pleasure

94

From the original in the Morgan Library, New York. Probably
Prince Hoare (1755-1834) sculptor and author, son of William
Hoare the portrait painter; made honorary Foreign Secretary of the
Royal Academy 1799; published *Academic Correspondence*, 1805; and
Academic Annals of Painting, 1805. The best known of his plays is
No Song, No Supper (Drury Lane, 1790)

The letter refers to Reynold's Fourth Discourse in which he considers
the grand style, which, in his view, should be used for history painting.
He contrasts it with the ornamental style which he associates with
Tintoretto and Veronese and their followers. "Though it be allowed
that elaborate harmony and colouring a brilliancy of tints, a soft
and gradual transition from one to another present to the eye
what an harmonious concert of music does to the ear, it must be
remembered that painting is not merely the gratification of sight."
The ornamental was in Sir Joshua's view a lower branch of painting
than history. Referring to portrait painting he says "those of us who
move in the humbler walks of the profession are not ignorant that as
the natural dignity of the subject is less, the more all the little
ornamental helps are necessary to its embellishment"

which a plump morsel, smoothly gliding through a narrow glib passage into the regions of bliss, and moistened with the dews of imagination, naturally creates. Some iron-faced dogs, you know, seem to chew dry ingratitude, and swallow discontent. Let such be kept to *under parts*, and never trusted to support a character. In all but eating, stick to Garrick; in *that* let him stick to you, for I'll be curst if you are not his master! Never mind the fools who talk of imitation and copying; all is imitation, and if you quit that natural likeness to Garrick which your mother bestowed upon you, you'll be flung. Ask Garrick else.

Why, Sir, what makes the difference, between man and man, is real performance, and not genius or conception. There are a thousand Garricks, a thousand Giardinis, and Fischers, and Abels. Why only one Garrick with Garrick's eyes, voice, &c.? One Giardini with Giardini's fingers, &c.? But one Fischer with Fischer's dexterity, quickness, &c.? Or more than one Abel with Abel's feeling upon the instrument? All the rest of the world are mere *hearers* and *see'rs*.

Now, as I said in my last, as Nature seems to have intended the same thing in you as in Garrick, no matter how short or how long, her kind intention must not be crossed. If it is, she will tip the wink to Madam Fortune, and you'll be kicked down stairs.

Think on that Master Ford.

God bless you,

Bath, 18th July, 1773   T.G.

46. TO MR. HOARE

Mr. Gainsborough's Respects to Mr. Hoare, and is much obliged for the sight of Sir Joshua's Discourse which he thinks amazingly clever, and cannot be too much admired (together with its Ingenious Author) by every candid lover of the Art. The truth of what he observes concerning Fresco, and the Great style, Mr. G. is convinced of by what he has often heard Mr. Hoare say of the works of Rafaelle and Michel Angelo—But betwixt Friends Sir Joshua either forgets, or does not chuse see that his Instruction is all adapted to form the History Painter, which he must know there is no call for in this country. The Ornamental style (as he calls it) seems form'd for Portraits. Therefore he had better come *down to Watteau* at once (who was a very fine Painter taking away the french conceit) and let us have a few Tints; or else why does Sir Joshua put tints equal to Painted Glass, only to make the People talk of Colors flying when the great style would do. Every one knows that the grand style must

From the original in the possession of The Historical Society of Pennsylvania

1 This is almost certainly Ozias Humphrey (1742–1810), who often accompanied Gainsborough on sketching expeditions near Bath. This letter is transcribed in J. H. Anderdon's interleaved copy of Edward's *Anecdotes of Painters*, volume 2, page 297, preserved in the Print Room at the British Museum. The transcription is pasted on the back of a letter to Ozias Humphrey from Opie, to whom he had written asking if he might make copies, a request which he refused as Gainsborough had done.

(I am indebted to John Hayes for this information)

From *Whitley* unpublished papers British Museum; sold Sotheby 28 February 1949, (157)

1 William Jackson (1730–1803) composer and organist, lay vicar and Master of Choristers at Exeter Cathedral. In 1798 published *The Four Ages*, together with Essays on various subjects including a *Character of Gainsborough*. His Cathedral Music was collected and published in 1820. In his spare time he painted landscapes under the influence of Gainsborough

2 *See* Letter *p.* 39

consist in plainness & simplicity, and that silks & satins, Pearls and trifling oranments would be as hurtfull to simplicity, as flourishes in a Psalm Tune; but Fresco would no more do for Portraits than an Organ would please Ladies in the hands of Fischer; there must be variety of lively touches and surprizing Effects to make the Heart dance, or else they had better be in a Church—so in Portrait Painting there must be a Lustre and finishing to bring it up to individual Life.

As Mr. G. hates of all things the least tendency to the sour Critic, hopes to talk over the affair some Evening over a Glass, as there is no other Friendly or sensible way of settling these matters except upon *Canvas*.

[*Unsigned and undated*]

47. MR. HUMPHREY[1]

Dear Sir,

I should be glad to lend you any of my Landskips to copy, did it not affect the sale of new Pictures, to have any copies taken of them, for which reason I have often been obliged to refuse, where it would have given me pleasure to oblige my friend

believe me

Dear Sir

Your most obedient

humble ser[t].

THO. GAINSBOROUGH

Friday morn.

48. TO WILLIAM JACKSON[1]

Dear Jackson,

I have outdone myself in a Letter to the Duke of Bedford,[2] the sketch of which perhaps you may see one time or other. I can draw a *character* better than I thought for, and I reckon upon the whole I have been lucky in the stile of the letter. If my single plumper will do anything, you'l hear soon, for I told the Duke where you Lodge. Let me hear soon from you

& believe me yours most

Sincerely

THO. GAINSBOROUGH

May 29th 1768

This and the following ten letters are taken from the originals at the Royal Academy

On the front of letter four William Jackson wrote "This parcel of letters are kept for my brother Thomas Jackson, if ever he returns to England but if not during my life they are to be burnt." On his return from Italy Thomas Jackson received the letters, which afterwards came into the possession of one of his great nieces, by whom they were sold to the Royal Academy about 1885

1 Mr. Palmer was the proprietor of the two theatres in Bath and his son John Palmer (1742–1818) was his agent in London

My Dear Jackson,

Will it (damn this Pen) will it serve as any apology for not answering your last obliging Letter to inform you that I did not receive it of near a Month after it arrived shut up in a Music Book at Mr. Palmer's[1] — I admire your notions of most things and do agree with you that there might be exceeding pretty Pictures painted of the kind you mention. But are you sure you don't mean instead of the flight into Egypt, my flight out of Bath! Do you consider my dear maggotty Sir, what a deal of work history Pictures require to what little dirty subjects of coal horses & jackasses and such figures as I full up with; no, you don't consider anything about that part of the story, you design faster than any man or any thousand men could Eexecute. There is but one *flight* I should like to paint and that's yours *out* of Exeter, for while your numerous & polite acquaintance encourage you to talk so cleverly, we shall have but few Productions, real & substantial Productions — But to be serious (as I know you love to be) do you really think that a regular Composition in the Landskip way should ever be fill'd with History, or any figures but such as fill a place (I won't say stop a Gap) or to create a little business for the Eye to be drawn from the Trees in order to return to them with more glee — I did not know that you admired those *tragicomic* Pictures, because some have thought that a regular History Picture may have too much background and the composition hurt by not considering what ought to be principle. But I talk now like old square toes there is no rule of that kind say you

But then say I

damme you lie!

If I had but room & time before Palmer seals up his packet I'd trim you — I have been riding out with him this morning. I wish I had been with him in Devonshire — Adieu   T.G.

Bath Augt. 23rd

My dear Jackson

To show you that I can be as quick as yourself tho: I shall never be half a quarter so clever, I am answering your letter the very moment I received it from Mr. Palmer — I shall not teaze you upon the subject of the *flight* as we are now upon a *better* & that which of all others I have long wished to touch upon; because tho I'm a rogue in talking upon Painting & love to *seem* to take things wrong, I can be both serious and honest upon any subjects thoroughly pleasing to

me—and such will ever be those wherein your happiness and our Friendship are concerned—let me then throw aside that damn'd *grinning trick* of mine for a moment and be as serious & stupid as a Horse. Mark then, that ever since I have been quite clear in your being a real Genius, so long have I been of opinion that you are dayly throwing your gift away upon *Gentlemen* & only studying how you shall become the *Gentleman* too—now damn Gentlemen, there is not such a set of Enemies to a real artist in the world as they are, if not kept at a proper distance. *They* think (and so may you for a while) that they reward your merit by their Company & notice; but I, who blow away all the chaff & by G—in their eyes too if they dont stand clear, know that they have but one part worth looking at, and that is their Purse; their Hearts are seldom near enough the right place to get a sight of it—If any gentleman comes to my House, my man asks them if they want me (provided they dont seem satisfied with seeing the Pictures) & then he askes *what* they would please to want with me; if they say a Picture, Sir please to walk this way and my Master will speak with you; but if they only want me to bow and compliment —Sir my Master is walk'd out—and so my dear there I nick them. Now if a *Lady* a handsome Lady comes tis as much as his Life is worth [torn page] send them away so—But this is [torn page] as you knew this before—[torn page] I wish you lived a little nearer so that I could see you often, or a good deal nearer if you please—I have no Acquaintance now, nor will I 'til I can say within myself *I approve my Choice.* There are but very few *clever* fellows worth hanging and that consideration makes you the more *worthy.*

Adieu for want of room & I'll write
again very soon

Bath Sept 2nd 1767 T.G.

51. TO WILLIAM JACKSON

My Dear Jackson

Now you seem to lay too much stress upon me, and show yourself to be a serious fellow. I question if you could splice all my Letters together whether you would find more connection and sense in them than in many Landskips joined where half a Tree was to meet half a Church to make a principal object. I should not think of my pretending to reproach you who are a regular system of Philosophy, a reasonable creature and a *particular Fellow.* If I meant anything (which God knows if I did) it was this, that many a *real Genius* is lost

in the fictitious Character of the Gentleman; and that as many of those creatures are continually courting you, possibly you might forget, what I without any merit to myself remember from mere shyness Namely that they make no part of the Artist. Depend upon it Jackson you have more sense in your little finger than I have in my whole Body and Head; I am the most inconsistent, changeable being, so full of fitts and starts, that if you mind what I say, it will be shutting your Eyes to some purpose.

I am only sensible of meaning, and of having once said, that I wish you lived nearer to me; but that this wish does not proceed from a selfishness rather than any desire of correcting any step of yours I much doubt—perhaps you can see that, though I cannot. I might add perhaps in my red hot way that damme Exeter is no more a place for a Jackson than Sudbury in Suffolk is for a G. But all the rest you know better than I can tell you I'm certain—you have one Fault which I must tell you of, you can stop to gaze with wonder and astonishment upon such a fellow as H—y and let slip all his merit of care, labour and president selfishnefs through your own fingers—tis mighty pretty to be sure to stand and admire another man hop upon one Leg, and forget the use of two *damned long ones*, think of that & Backer Longo [sic] think of that—why man you have as good a stock of Haberdashery about you as any of them all, if you had but the same hungry eyes to look about you—well after all Bath is a lively Place--not but [London?] is above all—you understhimble [sic] me [blot] hope no offence—

I look upon this letter as one of my most regular performances so don't let's have any of your airs—I could say a deal more but what can a man say pent up in a corner Thus; if you was a Lady I would say what I have often said in a corner by way of making the most of the last Inch. Yours up to the hilt

T.G.

Bath Sep. 14th

104

Plate 14
THE WATERING PLACE by Sir Peter Paul Rubens
National Gallery

Plate 15

105

DAVID GARRICK
Formerly Corporation of Stratford-on-Avon

Dear Jackson,

Is it true that you broke your Neck in going home? I have not seen Palmer but only the day after your departure to learn the truth. It is a current report here that the Great and the Aimable Mr. Jackson got a Mischief in going home, that you had tied your horse by the head so fast that his head was dragg'd off in going down a hill and that you ordered the driver (like a near sighted man) to go back for the horses body, and that the Chaise horses frightened at the sight of the boys riding up upon a Horse without a head took fright and made for Exeter—and that you unwilling to leave your Horse in that condition took a flying leap out at the window and pitched head foremost into a hollow tree. Miss d—l has heard this story, and says if it be true she'l never touch a Note again. I hope to hear from either Palmer or Bearing when I see them, some more favourable account of you. I'm but little disposed to pity you because you slip'd away so dam'd sly without giving me any more time than you had to jump into the hollow tree.

Pray if your damn'd long fingers escaped lets hear from you soon, and in the mean time I'll pray thats its all a lie

believe me Yours Sincerely

THO. GAINSBOROUGH

Bath Feb. 6th

Will you meet me at London anytime and I'll order Business accordingly.

Dear Jackson,

If your Neck is but safe, damn your Horse's head—I am so pleased with both your Remarks and your Indigo, that I know not which to admire most, or which to think most of immediate use; the Indigo you leave me in doubt whether there be any more to be got, whereas I am pretty sure of some more of your thoughts now we are fairly settled into a correspondence; your observations are like all yours, just natural, and not common—your Indigo is cleare like your understanding & pure as your Music, not to say exactly of the same Blue as that Heaven from whence all your ideas are reflected—to say the truth of your Indigo, 'tis delightful, so look sharp for some more (& I'll send you a drawing) and for your thoughts, I have often flattered myself I was just going to think so.

1 Probably the picture formerly in the collection of Lord Sackville at Knole and now in the Robert Sterling and Francine Clark Art Foundation, Williamstown, Massachusetts, U.S.A., *see E.K.W.* 801
These were the children of Thomas Linley the Musician, who was an intimate friend of Gainsborough. Mozart predicted that young Thomas (1756–78) had he lived would have been one of greatest ornaments of the musical world, *see Whitley p.* 390, and *E.K.W.* 447
Elizabeth, a singer married Richard Brinsley Sheridan
For portraits of her by Gainsborough, *see E.K.W.* 449, 450 *and* 613

The lugging in objects whether agreeable to the whole or not is a sign of the least Genius of anything, for a person able to collect in the mind will certainly groupe in the mind also; and if he cannot master a number of Objects so as to introduce them in friendship, let him do but a few—and that you know my Boy makes simplicity. One part of a Picture ought to be like the first part of a Tune; that you can guess what follows, and that makes the second part of the Tune and so I've done—

My respects to Mr. Tremlett, Bearing did not call upon me, I hear he's gone from Bath.

The Harp is packed up to come to you and you shall *take it out* with Miss— as I'll not *take* anything for it but give it to you to twang upon when you can't twang upon Mrs. Jackson, to whom pray my Comp^{ts} if there is no impropriety in the Introduction.

54. TO WILLIAM JACKSON

My dear Jackson,

I will suppose all you say about my Exhibition Pictures to be true because I have not time to dispute it with you—I am much obliged to you, and wish I could spend a few days with you in Town; but I have began a large Picture of Tommy Linley & his sister,[1] and cannot come—I suppose you know the Boy is bound for Italy the first opportunity. Pray do you remember carrying me to a Picture dealers somewhere by Hanover Square, and my being struck with the leaving and touch of a little bit of Tree; the whole Picture not above 8 or 10 Inches high and about a foot long. I wish if you have time that you'd enquire what it might be purchased for and give me one line more whilst you stay in Town.

If you can come this way home [blot] one may enjoy a day or two of your Company—I shall be heartily glad, I can always make up one Bed for a *Friend* without any trouble and nobody has a better Claim to that Title or a better title to that Claim than Yourself.

believe me Dear Jackson
Yours most sincerely
THO. GAINSBOROUGH

May 11th. 1768

My Compliments attend all enquiring Friends and damn this Pen.

1 John Dunning, First Baron Ashburton (1731–83). The leading lawyer of the day and Solicitor General in the Duke of Grafton's administration in 1768

My Dear Jackson,

I should have wrote to you sooner, but have been strangely hurried since I left Exeter—In my way home I met with Ld Shelburne, who insisted on my making them a short visit, and I don't regret going ('tho I generally do to all Lord's Houses as I met with Mr. Dunning[1] there). There is something exclusive of the clear and deep understanding of that Gentleman most exceedingly pleasing to me —He seems the only man who talks as Giardini plays, if you know what I mean; he puts no more motion than what goes to the real performance, which constitutes that ease & gentility peculiar to damn'd Clever Fellows, each in their way. I observe his Forhead jets out, and mine runs back a good deal more than common, which accounts for some difference betwixt our *Parts*—no doubt, with me, but he has an uncommon share of Brains and those disposed so as to overlook all the rest of his *Parts*, let them be ever so powerful. He is an amazing *compact* Man in every respect; and as we get a sight of everything by comparison only think of the difference betwixt Mr. Dunning almost motionless, with a Mind brandishing, like Lightening, from corner to corner of the Earth, whilst a Long cross made fellow only flings his arms about like thrashing flails without half an Idea of what he would be at—and besides this neatness in outward appearance, his Store-Room seems cleared of all french ornaments and gingerbread work, everything is simplicity and elegance & in its proper place; no disorder or confusion in the *furniture* as if he was going to remove. Sober sense and great acuteness are marked very strong in his Face, but if these were all, I should only admire him as a great Lawyer; but there is a Genius (in our sense of the word) shines in all he says— In short Mr. Jackson of Exeter, I begin to think there is something in the air of Devonshire that grows Clever fellows I could name 4 or 5 of you, superior to the product of any other County in England.

Pray make my Compliments to one Lady who is *neat about the Mouth* if you can guess & believe me most faithfully.

Yours

THO. GAINSBOROUGH

Bath Sepr. 2nd

Plate 16
THE HARVEST WAGGON (DETAIL)
Barber Institute of Fine Art, Birmingham

Plate 17
JOHANN CHRISTIAN FISCHER (1733–1800)
By gracious permission of Her Majesty the Queen

56. TO WILLIAM JACKSON

115

My Dear Jackson,

I am much obliged to you for your last Letter, and the Lessons recd. before; I think I now begin to see a little into the nature of Modulation and the introduction of flats and sharps; and when we meet you shall hear me play extempore—My Friend Abel has been to visit me, but he made but a short stay, being obliged to go to Paris for a Month or six weeks, after which He has promised to come again. There never was a poor Devil so fond of Harmony, with so little knowledge of it, so that what you have done is pure Charity—I dined with Mr. Duntze in expectation (and indeed full assurance) of hearing your scholar Miss Floud play a little, but was for the second time *flung*. She had best beware of the third time, lest I *fling* Her, and if I do I'll have a Kiss before she is up again. I'm sick of Portraits and wish very much to take my Viol da Gamba and walk off to some sweet Village when I can paint Landskips and enjoy the fag End of Life in quietness and ease. But these fine Ladies and their Tea drinkings, Dancings, *Husband huntings* and such will fob me out of the last ten years, & I fear miss getting Husbands too—But we can say nothing to these things you know Jackson, we must jogg on and be content with the jingling of the Bells, only d–mn it I hate a dust, the Kicking up of a dust, and being confined *in Harness* to follow the track, whilst others ride in the waggon, under cover, stretching their Legs in the straw at Ease, and gazing at Green Trees & Blue skies without half my *Taste*, that's damn'd hard. My Comfort is, I have 5 Viols da Gamba 3 Jayes and two Barak Normans.

Adieu dear Jackson
and believe me ever & sincerely yours

Bath June 4th

THO. GAINSBOROUGH

57. TO WILLIAM JACKSON

Dear Jackson,

Methinks I hear you say, all Friendship is my [word crossed out] and all sincerity my [word crossed out] only because I have not had time since my hurry of finishing two full lengths & a Landskip for the Exhibition, to answer your last two Letters—But don't be in hurry to determine anything about *me*, if you are, ten to one you are wrong—those who can claim a longer acquaintance with me than Mr. Jackson knowing at this moment but very little of my real temper. I'm heartily sorry that you don't come to reside nearer Bath as you expected not because you are disapointed of the advantages of Conversing with me and my Works, but because I am deprived of

much greater advantages of sucking your sensible skull, and of the opportunity I might possibly have of convincing you how much I shall always esteem your various and extensive Talents, not to mention what I think still better worth mentioning, namely your honesty & undesigning plainness & openess of Soul. They say your mind is not *Worldly*, no said I, because its *heavenly*—I think a tollerable reason Master Mathews.

I fear my Lad I shall have it this Exhibition for never was such slight dabs presented to the Eyes of a Million, but I grow dauntless not of Meer stupidity as I grow old, and I believe any one that plods on in any one way, especially if that one way will bring him bread & cheese as well as a better, will grow the same.

You mentioned something you had committed to paper upon Painting, I hope you have not committed Painting upon the same paper, because you know I am to see it. Mr. Palmer was going to London the last time I saw him so I fear it may be some time before you receive this Letter, but as soon as you do shew how well you can forgive by a speedy answer. The Harp is come back and I'm sorry you thought it worth the [letter torn] pains of returning as the Lady was not [letter torn] of it—I suppose you had played upon her ti'l you was tired and so could not let her have it—thanks for the Indigo a little of it goes a great way, which is lucky Adieu dear Jackson, and believe me most sincerely yours,

THO. GAINSBOROUGH

respects to Mr. Tremlet.

58. TO MR. WILLIAM JACKSON, EXETER

Dear Jackson,

I will confess to you that I think it unpardonable in me not to speak seriously upon a subject of so much consequence as that which has employd us of late; therefore you shall now have my thoughts without any humming swearing or affectation of wit—Indeed my Affection for you would naturally have led me that way before now, but that I am soon lost if I pretend to reasoning; and you being all regularity and Judgment, I own provoke me the more to break loose; as he who cannot be correct, is apt to divert the Eye with a little freedom of handling but no more of it. I must own your calculations & comparison betwixt our different professions to be just provided you remember that in mine a Man may do great things and starve in a Garret if he does not conquer his Passions and conform to the *Common Eye* in chusing that branch which *they* will encourage & pay

for. Now there cannot be that difference betwixt Music & Painting unless you suppose that the Musician Voluntarily shuns the only profitable branch, and will be a Chamber Counsel when he might appear at the Bar. You see I'm out of my subject already. But now in again. If Music will not satisfye you without a *Certainty* (which by the by is nonsense, begging your pardon, for there is no such thing in any profession), then I say be a *Painter*—You have more of the painter than half those that get money by it, that I will swear, if you desire it, upon a Church Bible. You want a little drawing and the use of pencil and colours which I could put into your hand in one month, without meddling with your head; I propose to let that alone, if you'll let mine off easy. There is a branch of Painting next in profit to Portrait and quite in your power without any more drawing than I'll answer for your having, which is Drapery & Landskip backgrounds. Perhaps you don't don't know that whilst a Face painter is harrased to death the drapery painter sits and earns 5 or 6 hundred a year, and laughs all the while—

Your next will be to tell me, what I know as well as yourself, viz that I'm an impertinent Coxcomb—this I know, & will speak out if you kill me for it, you are too modest too diffident too sensible & too honest ever to push in Music [five words are crossed out].

Sincerely T.G.

59. TO WILLIAM SHAKESPEARE JACKSON ESQ AT EXETER

Dear Jackson,

I thought you was sick as I had not seen you for some Days, and last night when I went to the Play in hopes of meeting you there, Mr. Palmer confirmed my fears; I fully intended putting on my thick shoes this morning, but have been hindered by some *Painter Plagues*; pray send me word whether there is any occasion for Doctor Moysey to come to you, in *Palmer's opinion*, damn your own, for you are much too like me to know how it is with you. The Doctor shall come in a moment if there is the least occasion and I know he will with pleasure without your touching your breeche's pocket. I'll be with you soon to feel your pulse myself.

So God mend you.

T. GAINSBOROUGH

Tuesday Morning.

I have spoilt a fine piece of drawing paper for you because I had no other at hand, and in a hurry to know how you are

From the original in the possession of Mr. Gerard Mackworth Young. Mr. Young's forbear, Sir Samuel Young, and William Jackson's son married sisters – daughters of Charles Baring of Exmouth, and the letter has never passed out of the Jackson, Baring and Young families. *See* Marcus Whiffen, *Burl. Mag.*, February 1942, *p.* 46

1 Portrait of Jackson shown at R.A. 1770, *see E.K.W.* 398

Dear Jackson,

I suppose I never draw a Portrait half so like the sitter, as my silence since the receipt of your last resembles Neglect & Ingratitude, owing to two of the crossest accidents that ever attended a poor fiddler. First and most unfortunately, I have been 4 times after Bach, and have never laid Eyes on Him; and secondly, and most provokingly, I have had a Parcell made up of two Drawings and a Box of Pencils, such as you wrote for, ever since the Day after I recd your favor inclosing the *Tenths*, and directed for you to go by the Exeter Coach, which has laid in my Room by the neglect of two blockheads one my Nephew, who is too proud to carry a bundle *under his arm*, though his betters the Journeymen Taylors always carry their foul shirts so; and my d . . mnd cowardly footman who forsooth is afraid to peep into the street for fear of being press'd for sea service, the only service God almighty made him for—so that, my dear Jackson, if it was not for your being endow'd with Jobe's Patience I should think myself deservedly for ever shut out of your favor; but surely I shall catch Bach soon to get you an answer to your Letter; and for the Drawings if I don't carry them myself to the inn to-morrow.

There is a Letter of nonsense enclosed with the Drawings to plague you once more about 6ths and 10ths—which you may read as you hap to be in humour when you see the Drawings—til then I'm sure you can't bear the sight of my odious Hand,
so no more at present as the saying is
but yours sincerely
T. G.

Pall Mall

You hear I suppose that all Lords and Members have given up their privilege of franking to ease the Taxes, I'm sorry for it.
Jan: 25th 1777

no haste

My dear Jackson,

I have been most *unaccountably* hindered from writing to you, from time to time and I flatter myself as that is really the case you'l think me a clever fellow for not endeavouring to *account* for it. I saw you at the Exhibition,[1] and as I expected hung a mile high. I wish you had been a created Lord before my sending the Picture,

2 *See* Letter *p.* 29
3 *See* Letter to Unwin *p.* 167

From the original in the possession of Major Norman Leith-Hay-Clark
1 Edmund Garvey? 1813. Landscape painter, exhibited R.A. 1770
and became a full member in 1783, he specialised in views of Gentlemen's Seats. *A View of Plymouth Dock*, 1788, is in the Diploma Gallery
at the Royal Academy

then that puppy Newton[2] would have taken care you had been in sight. I wonder if any of your acquaintance knew you besides myself! This I'll swear, they none of them know your Rogues tricks half so well as I do, and yet at the same time Value you for your honesty. I believe I shall come this Autumn to Exmouth to bathe in order to *stand* next Winter. My wife seems coming into the scheem.

Let me know if I must send you your Head, or whether you can do with the half one you already are in possession of none but a half-headed fool would pay you this Compliment—mark that—and make my Compliments to the Sensible and agreeable Mr. Tremlet; If I come I'll plague Him enough I'll warrant you.

Well, God bless you, I can't think of any more Nonsense and you don't admit of *Drawing* in Letters, or else I could add a trifle more for your amusement.

believe me Dear Jackson
Ever yours
THO. GAINSBOROUGH

Bath June 9th 1770

Observe the reason I have not answered your last sooner I have been 3 months from home, at Mr. George Pitts Country House.[3]

62. TO MR. WILLIAM JACKSON

Dear Jackson,

The Gentleman who brings you this, is Mr Garvey[1] an excellent Landskip Painter and particular Friend of mine, who lives in Bath

He is no stranger to Mr Jackson's merit, tho' to his Person and wishes to be acquainted with one, so fond of Landskip, and so able a performer in his own branch of Painting—Pray shew him something of your doing, and get him a sight of whatever is worth his seeing in Exeter. I hope to see you in about a fortnight, as I purpose spending a month or six weeks at Tingmouth or other places round Exeter—get your Chalks ready, for we must draw together—Excuse haste and believe me, Dear Sir yours most truly

THOS. GAINSBOROUGH

Bath July 8th 1779

From *Whitley*, unpublished papers in the British Museum

1 Kirby, John Joshua (1716–74), settled in Ipswich in 1738 as coach and house painter, there he met Gainsborough. Later moved to London, and in 1768 became President of the Society of Artists; was made Clerk of the Works at Kew Palace by George III

2 Gainsborough had received a letter from Reynolds asking him to become one of the original members of the R.A. founded by royal instrument in 1768

From the original in the possession of Mrs. Clarabut.

1 William Pearce (1751–1842). According to Whitley Pearce was for some years Chief Clerk to the Admiralty, and an amateur of literary tastes. *See Whitley p.* 393. For his portrait by Gainsborough, *see E.K.W.* 538

2 Sam Kilderbee

3 Dr. Brown whose name Gainsborough couples with the poet Thomas Gray was Dr. John Brown, D.D., Vicar of Newcastle who published *A Description of the Lake at Keswick (and the adjacent country) in Cumberland* in 1772, and a long letter in the *Monthly Ledger* in 1775 extolling the picturesque charms of Derwentwater

63. TO MR. KIRBY[1] AT THE SOCIETY OF ARTISTS
TURKS HEAD GERRARD ST., SOHO

Mr. President & Gentlemen, Directors of the Society of Artists of Great Britain

I thank you for the honour done me in appointing me one of your Directors, but for a particular reason[2] I beg leave to resign, and am gentlemen, your most obliged & obedient & Humble Servant

THOS. GAINSBOROUGH

Bath December 5th, 1768

64. TO WILLIAM PEARCE[1] KEW GREEN,

Dear Sir

I don't know if I told you that I'm going along with a Suffolk Friend[2] to visit the Lakes in Cumberland & Westmorland; and purpose when I come back to show you that your Grays and Dr. Brownes[3] were tawdry fan-Painters. I purpose to mount all the Lakes at the next Exhibition, in the great stile; and you know if the People don't like them, 'tis only jumping into one of the deepest of them from off a wooded Island, and my reputation will be fixd for ever.

I took the liberty of sending you a little Perry out of Worstershire, and when the weather settles in hot again, should be much obliged if you and Mrs. P........ would drink a little of it and fancy it Champaign for my sake. I doubt whether I can shake you by the hand before I go, but when I come back, I'll shake you by the collar, if you'l promise to keep you hands still.

Believe me Dear Sir most sincerely yours

THO. GAINSBOROUGH

Kew Green Sunday morn, Church Time

65. TO WILLIAM PEARCE

My dear Pearce,

I am extremely obliged to you and Mrs. Pearce for your kind enquiries; I hope I am now getting better, as the swelling is considerably increased and more painful. We have just received some cheeses from Bath, and beg the favor of you to accept two of them.

My dear Pearce,

Ever yours sincerely

THOS. GAINSBOROUGH

Wed Morning
[*1788*]

From *Fulcher p.* 147

From the original in the Morgan Library, New York

1 Sir William Johnstone Pulteney (1729–1805) possibly exhibited R.A. 1772, *see E.K.W.* 565

From the original at the Royal Academy

1 *The Woodman.* Painted in the summer of 1787 was burnt in the fire at Lord Gainsborough's house, Exton Park, in 1810, *see E.K.W.* 806
There is in the museum at Leicester a full-size needlework picture by Miss Linley of this picture

From *Whitley*, unpublished papers British Museum; sold Sotheby 24th June, 1924, 295(5)

1 The picture *Girl with Pigs* is now at Castle Howard, *see E.K.W.* 799
In a postscript to a letter written to Lord Ossory by Reynolds about a supposed Titian, he says "I am thinking what picture to offer in Exchange – what if I give Gainsborough's Pigs for it is by far the best Picture he ever Painted or perhaps ever will", *see* F. W. Hilles, *Letters of Sir Joshua Reynolds*, Cambridge University Press 1929, *p.* 154

66. TO MR. PULTENEY[1]

Sir,

I generally view my Works of a Sunday tho. I never touch; and I think we could still finish a little higher, to great advantage, if it would not be intruding too much upon your good nature to bestow one more little sitting of about half an hour, either tomorrow morning or any other most agreeable to yourself. I am fired with the thoughts of Mrs. Pulteney's giving me leave to send you to the Royal Exhibition, and of making a good Portrait of you, therefore hope Sir, you will be so good to pardon my giving you all this trouble.

I am

Sir your most obliged &
most obedient humble servant
THO. GAINSBOROUGH

Circus
Sunday evening

67. TO SIR JOSHUA REYNOLDS

Dear Sir Joshua

I am just to write what I fear you will not read after lying in a dying state for 6 months. The extreme affection which I am informed of by a Friend which Sir Joshua has expresd induces me to beg a last favor, which is to come once under my Roof and look at my things, my woodman[1] you never saw, if what I ask (now?) is not disagreeable to youd feeling that I may have the honor to speak to you. I can from a sincere Heart say that I always admired and sincerely loved Sir Joshua Reynolds.

THO. GAINSBOROUGH

68. TO SIR JOSHUA REYNOLDS

Sir Joshua,

I think myself highly honour'd and much obliged to you for this singular mark of your favour: I may truly say I have brought my Piggs[1] (sic) to a fine market.

Dear Sir,

Your ever obliged and obedient servant.
THO. GAINSBOROUGH

Plate 18
LETTER TO THOMAS HARVEY
University of London, Courtauld Institute

Dear Sir,

Your very obliging Letter inclosing a Norwich Bank Bill, Value seventy three Pounds, on Mess.rs Vere & Williams, I acknowledge (when Rd.) to be in full for the Landscape with Cows & all demands.

I am glad Sir, that the Picture got no damage; if ever you should find anything of a Chill come upon the Varnish of my Pictures, owing to its being a Spirit of Wine Varnish, take a rag, or little bit of sponge with Nut oil, and rub it til the mist clears away, and then wipe as much of it off as a few strokes with a clean Cloth – ^will effect this done once or twice a year after damp weather you will find convenient – – My Swelled Neck is got very painful indeed, but I hope it be near coming to a Cure – How happy should I be to set out for Yarmouth and after recruiting my poor Crazy Frame, enjoy the coasting along til I reached Norwich and give you a call – God only knows what is for me, but hope is the Pallet of Colors we all paint with in sickness –

tis odd how all the Childish passions hang about one in sickness, I feel such a fondness for my first imitations of little Dutch Landskips that I can't keep from working an hour or two of a Day, though with a great mixture of bodily Pain – I am so childish that I could make a Kite, catch Gold Finches, or build little Ships –

Believe me Dear Sir
with the greatest sincerity
Your ever Obliged & Obedient
Servant

Pall Mall
May 22d 1788 –

Tho Gainsborough

P.S. I have recollected that a Stamp Rect. may be proper.

Thomas Harvey Esq.r
at Catton near
Norwich

5

3 · 06
2 · 6
1 · 18

Plate 19

129

THE COTTAGE DOOR

Henry E. Huntingdon Library and Art Gallery

From the original in the British Museum

1 Philip Lord Royston (1720–96) later Second Earl of Hardwicke, *see* *E.K.W.* 350

2 Quin, James (1693–1766). Actor, born in Dublin where he played in his early days, later appeared at Drury Lane and Covent Garden, where in 1746 and 1747 he was the rival of Garrick. He retired in 1751. Horace Walpole admired him more than Garrick

3 Moysey, Dr. Abel (1715–80). For portrait by Gainsborough, *see* *E.K.W.* 505

69. RECEIPT FOR REYNOLD'S PAYMENT FOR THE GIRL WITH PIGS

April 20th, 1782 Received of Sir Joshua Reynolds one hundred guineas in full for a picture of 'A girl with Piggs' & all demands £105.

THOMAS GAINSBOROUGH

70. TO LORD ROYSTON[1]

My Lord,

I should have answered your Lordship's obliging Letter sooner but was from home when it came and returned but yesterday. I am now about your Lordship's Picture and shall spare no pains to make it as good a Picture as I possibly can; but for fear I should not be able to compleat it time enough for Lord Hardwick to have into the Country when His Lordship leaves Town, I should be much obliged if your Lordship would be pleased to give orders that it may not be open'd in London, but forwarded immediately on its arrival, into the Country as I shall paper it up to secure the dust from lodging on the surface of the Picture. The payment of the remainder of the Money would be soon enough when your Lordship comes again to Bath; But, if your Lordship should be uneasy 'til the Debt is discharged, Mr. Hoare Banker at Temple Bar will give a proper Receipt in my Name.

His Grace the duke of Devonshire left Bath about 3 weeks since, and Mr. Quin,[2] told me he himself was going to Chatsworth to stay a few weeks. Dr. Moisy[3] has had a severe fit of the ague, and (as I am told) says he should make himself very easey with the loss of his Money if he could get rid of the ague; But whether the loss of the Money might not bring on a shaking fit that form'd itself into an Ague I must leave.

I am your Lordship's most obedient & most obliged humble servant

THO. GAINSBOROUGH

Bath, July 21st. 1763

From the original in the possession of the Earl of Sandwich, who published it in *The Times*, 27th January, 1955, together with a photograph of the portrait

1 John, Fourth Earl of Sandwich (1718–92), painted by Gainsborough and exhibited R.A. 1783 (190), *see E.K.W.* 599

2 Portrait of Queen Caroline

3 Ralph Edwards in a letter to *The Times* of 2nd March, 1955, suggests that the reference to the young man's performance may indicate the picture to be a copy by Dupont who was at that time thirty years of age. It is, as he points out, unlikely that Gainsborough would have made a copy of an earlier State portrait of Caroline of Anspach for the Corporation of Huntingdon even if the Fourth Earl paid the bill

Taken from a copy of the original letter transcribed in the Minutes of the Royal Society of Arts dated 13th December, 1775. Other Minutes of the Society are relevant:

6th December, 1775: "that Gainsborough should be approached as Nathaniel Dance has done nothing for two years although he had had the picture by Hudson for that period"

30th October, 1776: "The Secretary reported the painting had been delivered"

6th November, 1776: "ordered that Gainsborough should be paid 100 guineas which 'is the price he usually charges for a whole length picture'"

Dance was originally commissioned to paint a posthumous portrait of Lord Folkestone based on the three-quarter length portrait painted by T. Hudson in 1749 in the collection of Lord Radnor. It was to be "a whole length portrait drawn in the proper Coronation robes and the same size as the portrait of Lord Romney". Lord Romney was the second president of the Society. *See Whitley p.* 125 and *E.K.W.* 261

1 Jacob, First Viscount Folkestone (1694–1761). First President of the Society of Arts from 1755 until his death in 1761, *see E.K.W.* 261

71. TO THE EARL OF SANDWICH[1]

My Lord,—Dash'd entirely out of countenance this evening by the receipt of your Lordship's letter, I have nothing left but to hope and pray that the assembly may not happen till the latter end of the week; the dampness of the weather having been such, that the confounded paint would not dry so as to bear rolling up before Saturday night; on Sunday morning my servant saw the case put into the waggon; so I hope the picture[2] will be at Huntingdon near as soon as your Lordship will receive this letter. I have not a word to say as to the young man's performance;[3] but hope that if your Lordship should not think it well enough for the intended purpose, that your Lordship's cook maid will hang it up as her own Portrait in the kitchen and get some sign-post gentleman to rub out the crown and sceptre and put her on a blue apron, and say it was painted by G—who was very near being King's Painter only Reynold's Friends stood in the way.

I am

your Lordship's

most obedient and very humble

servant.

THO. GAINSBOROUGH

Monday Nov. 29th, 1784

72. TO THE SOCIETY OF ARTS

Sir

Agreeable to the obliging Order of the Society for a full length of the late Lord Folkestone,[1] I will take particular care to Execute it in my best manner and to get it done by the beginning of October next

I am Sir

Your much obliged and obedient Serv.

THOS. GAINSBOROUGH

Pall Mall
Dec. 11. 1775

134

Taken with the following three letters from an article by Granville Fell, *Connoisseur*, Vol. XCVIII, 1936, *p. 210 et seq*, where the portrait of Mrs. Awse is reproduced in colour, *see* also *E.K.W.* 24

The portrait was painted in Bath to the order of the sitter's brother Mr. Richard Stevens who was M.P. for Winscott, Torrington

Sir,

The least I can do when told of my faults in a genteal and friendly manner, is to acknowledge them, and ask pardon: I was tempted to exceed the bounds of good manners in keeping Mrs. Awse so long as my situation now requires all the *sail* I can crowd: the truth is Sir, I suffered some hardships in the first part of my Voyage and fancying now that I see *Land* makes me forget myself. I will send it immediatly and happy I shall be if you think the care & pains I have taken in the finishing part at all compensates for my faults in other respects.

I had the Frames made at the time I received your first Letter with the Drawing, and though doubtless there may appear some small difference upon immediate comparison with that it is design'd to match, yet the dimensions being pretty exact, I hope it will pass, especially Sir whilst the Eyes of your Friends are employ'd in admiring the Excellence of my Performances. I wish I could make you laugh till you forget how deficient I have been in point of good manners.

I hope Sir, the more I have punished you, the less pain you will suffer from the Gout, Methinks I could with pleasure bear a pinch in my Toe for you.

I am
(hoping Mrs. Awse is well)
Sir your Obedient humble Serv-
THO. GAINSBOROUGH

Circus,
Bath, Sept. 13th, 1767

P.S. I believe Sir it would astonish you to see how the new Buildings are extending in all points from the old center of Bath, The Pump Rooms—We almost reach Landsdown & Cleverton—down, north & south, but not quite to Bristol & London for East & West. I think verily the End of some of our *Master* Builders will be to meet some of their Marylebone Friends near a certain Ditch. It does not appear to me that many of the new Houses are occupied by Genteal Families newly residing in Bath, but only that the Lodging-House *Cats* are endeavouring to draw more Talons upon us, by having Houses in all quarters.

Plate 20
THE BOY IN THE CART (DRAWING)
British Museum

Plate 21
GIRL WITH PIGS
George Howard Esq.

Acco.ᵗ between Mᵣ. Thomas Gainsborough & Mᵣ. James Unwin

Ja:ˢ Unwin . . . Dr.		Gainsba Cr.	
1757		1757	
June 30 To Cash rec'd from his Grace		June 30. By Cash to Edwᵈ Wheeler Esq.	
the Duke of Beaufort Estate for 2 } 400 . . .		for prem: on Bond - - - -	360 . . .
years Annuity due Midsˢ 1757		By dᵒ. to dᵒ. for ⅔ year and 128 days	
		Intᵗˢ from 22ᵈ of Jany 1755 to this }	35 . 5 . 2
		day	
Novᵣ 13ᵗʰ 1757		By Cash pᵈ Mar: 5. 1756 for 5 yꝛˢ	
		Dividends on 3 poliys of forfeit }	19 . 19 . .
Recᵈ of Mr James Unwin the above Ballance		By dᵒ. paid Novᵣ 8 for 2 yꝛˢ dᵒ	7 . 13 .
of thirty seven pounds two shillings & ten			—————————
pence in full of all Demands			362 . 17 . 2
		Ballᵃ due from Mᵣ. Unwin }	
Tho: Gainsborough		to Mr Gainsborough - - - }	37 . 2 . 10
			—————————
			400 . - . -

Plate 22
ACCOUNT BETWEEN MR. THOMAS GAINSBOROUGH AND MR. JAMES UNWIN
British Museum

74. TO MR. RICHARD STEVENS, M.P.

Sir,

I hope by this time you have received Mrs. Awfe's Picture, and that it meets with your approbation. I this morning paid the Frame-maker, and am sorry to say that I think it a dear one, but he says the trouble he had in working after a limited scale and pattern in Drawing Occupied the additional charge; he set it at four Guineas, and for 3 Guineas & ½ I have the Burnish'd Gold sort. However if you, Sir, think it dear too I shall be willing to become a fellow sufferer as My Profits in the Portrait way is a little upon apothecray order—I shall be glad to hear it comes safe to hand, and suits pretty well with the other.

I am Sir your most obedient Servt

THO. GAINSBOROUGH

Bath,
Oct. 2nd 1767

I hope the Gout has left you & that Mrs. Awfe is well.

P.S.

Packing Case cost me 7 shillings which my Wife desires me always to remember and I often forget voluntarily because I'm afraid to mention it.

75. TO MR. RICHARD STEVENS, M.P.

Sir,

I have recd. the favor of your inclosing a Bill Value £15 which when pd. I acknowledge to be in full for Mrs. Awfe's Picture and Frame & all Demands.

I am sorry Sir I have not been so happy in Mrs. Awfe's Picture as to give satisfaction to yourself & Friends, but I believe nobody can always succeed alike at all times. I can only say it was not for want of either pains or Inclination; & as to the Frame it was done after the Drawing you sent, by the best frame-maker at Bristol. If at any time you should have a convenience of bringing Mrs. Awfe's Picture with you to Bath I shall very willingly make any alterations which you or Mrs. Awfe may think proper, without any additional charge—and am Sir Your most Obedient & humble Servant

THO. GAINSBOROUGH

Bath, Jan. 28th, 1768

P.S. I am extremely sorry for your long confinement but hope now you'l be free from the Gout for some years—

1 *See E.K.W.* 634

From the original in the Henry E. Huntingdon Library, California
1 Later Second Earl Aldborough, *see E.K.W.* 10

76. FRAGMENT OF A LETTER REFERRING TO THE PORTRAIT OF MR. RICHARD STEVENS,[1] M.P.

I have put it into the sort of Frame which you was pleased to order, which comes to two Guineas; the picture ten Guineas, and the Case seven shillings, in all twelve pounds nineteen shillings.

I am Sir your most Obedient humble Servant

THO. GAINSBOROUGH

Bath, April 13th, 1762

77. TO THE HON. EDWARD STRATFORD[1]

Dear Sir,

When you mention *Exhibition Pictures*, you touch upon a string, which once broke, all is at an End with me; but I do assure you, nay I swear by Saint Luke's Pencil, I have not dress'd nor sent a finished half length out of my doors since yours have been in hand so that I beg you to have patience to hear me, and I beg Mrs. Stratford to keep you in good nature for a moment, I do solemnly promise you to finish your Pictures in my best manner before any other from this time. I was obliged to cobble up something for the Exhibition or else (so far from being knighted) I should have been expel'd the Society, and have been look'd upon as a deserter, unworthy my *Diploma* sign'd with the King's own hand, which I believe you have seen most beautifully framed & hung up in my Painting-Room, *behind the Door*. Do good Sir let me know for certain when you think of returning home from abroad and if I disappoint you of *seeing* your Pictures hung in their Places *with my own Eyes*, I'll give you leave to boil me down for Painters Drying oil, and shiver my Bones into Pencil Sticks—could Shakespeare with his Mother Madam fancy say more—I wish you would recollect that Painting & Punctuality mix like Oil & Vinegar, & that Genius & regularity are utter Enemies, & must be to the end of Time—I would not insinuate that *I* am a genius any further than as I resemble one in your Opinion, who think I have no such thing as punctuality about me—In short Sir, I throw myself at your Feet, & thank God most sincerely that I am not any nearer to them, for surely you could not help kicking me—However Sir depend upon this, that I am most sincerely,

Your ever obedient & humble Servant

THO. GAINSBOROUGH

Bath May 1st. 1772

From the original in the Henry E. Huntingdon Library, California
Written on a letter card

From the original in the Houghton Library, Harvard University, in the Locker-Warburg Album, presented to the Library by Mr. and Mrs. Grimson

1 &2 These cannot be identified

Fulcher p. 186 gives five whole lengths as exhibited at the R.A. in 1771. Lady Sussex, Lord and Lady Ligonier, Mr. Nuthall and Captain Wade

3 *See E.K.W. pp.* 10 *and* 11

4 Gainsborough secured no footing at Court until 1780

Mr. Gainsborough presents his comp[ts] to Mr. Stratford; He does not understand whether Mr. Stratford means to have the Dog painted separate by Monsieur Dupont, or again put into Mrs. Stratford's Picture to spoil it; so cannot say anything about it to Day.

But with regard to Mrs. Stratford's Drawing, Mr. G- will expect the honor of seeing Mrs. Stratford to morrow Evening (*Dress'd*) at any hour agreeable to Mrs. Stratford.

79. TO THE HON[ble] MR. STRATFORD

Sir:

I had the honor of your obliging Letter last night, and sent the inclosed both as directed, and to one of them you have the enclosed Answ[r]. I am sorry you have had so much trouble in the affair you mention, 'tho I understood by the newspapers that you had recovered the Plate & Jewells, and that the Rascals were hang'd out of the way, as they richly desrved.

I am daubing away for the Exhibition with all my might, and have done two large Landskips[1] which will be in two handsome frames (exclusive of 3 full length Portraits)[2] and think, whether you have recovered your Riches or not, you ought to purchase them, because you have enough left, and the Landskips are the best I ever did, & probably will be the last I shall live to do. I wish that yours and Mrs. Stratfords Portraits[3] had been whole lengths that I might have Exhibited you, & have got Credit; but half lengths are overlook'd in such a monstrous large Room and at a Miles Distance.

I'm sorry your Chalk Drawings got Rubb'd as they were muzzy enough at first, as indeed all Chalk Drawings of Portraits must be so small and the Chalk so soft—I shall very willingly retouch them or do anything else for you, when I come to Town well knowing that if ever I am Knighted or have anything to do at St. James's[4] it must be through your Interest and singular Friendship for me—You may depend upon my utmost care to do every thing [to] your Pictures according to your direction and that you shall have them as soon as those Exhibition Pictures are packed up which will be in a Week. I beg my humble service to Mrs. Stratford I am

Sir your most obedient and humble
Servant

Bath March 21st 1771   THO. GAINSBOROUGH

Written on the back of the letter:

Pardon the vulgar form of this letter, occasioned by the unlucky shape of the card inclosed.

From the original, in 1934 in the possession of Mr. H. S. Marsham-Townshend, Scadbury Park

1 *See E.K.W.* 670

From the original in the Morgan Library, New York

1 Thicknesse, Philip (1719–92). Began life as an apothecary, went out to Georgia with Oglethorpe in 1733; served as a lieutenant in Jamaica against runaway negroes; in 1753 bought the governorship of Landguard Fort near Ipswich, where he met and befriended Gainsborough. He was imprisoned for libel, settled in Bath in 1768 and in 1784 erected in his grounds the first monument to Chatterton. Author of Memoirs, books on travel and pamphlets, and published privately the first biography of Gainsborough in 1788

80. TO CAPT. TOWNSHEND AT THOMAS TOWNSHEND'S ESQR. IN OLD BURLINGTON STREET, LONDON

Sir

I am sorry that from the nature of my dam'd Business, the Time of my coming to Town remains yet uncertain. But you may depend upon it, when I do, will wait on your sister & make the alterations She shall think necessary in your Picture.[1] I would not have you trouble yourself to pay Gossett, but let it alone till your return; I assure you, Sir, that's the least of my thoughts, since if I had never heard your Name, your Countenance I should think security for more than I shall ever get by Painting. I am Sir Your most obedient humble servant

THO. GAINSBOROUGH

Bath, April 22nd 1762

81. TO PHILIP THICKNESSE[1]

My dear Sir

I could not go to the play to-night until I had relieved my mind by sending you the enclosed banknote, and beg you will transit it to the afflicted woman by to-night's post.—Yours sincerely,

THOMAS GAINSBOROUGH

The group of letters printed below to Gainsborough's attorney James Unwin of Castle Yard, Holborn, was published by Sydney E. Harrison, "New Light on a Gainsborough Mystery", Connoisseur, January and February, 1922 (pp. 3–108, 87–91), together with twelve orders or drafts for payment from Gainsborough to Unwin and two of Unwin's accounts. The chief interest of the latter (Pl. 22) is that it shows the source of an annuity paid to Gainsborough on behalf of his wife from the Duke of Beaufort, which helped to clear up the mystery of Margaret Gainsborough's birth. This was confirmed by an entry in the Faringdon Diary published in the Morning Post, *28th February, 1922, according to which, Gainsborough's daughter told Faringdon that her Mother was a natural daughter of Henry, Duke of Beaufort, who settled £200 a year upon her, see S. E. Harrison,* Connoisseur, *April, 1922.*

1 Captain Thomas Saumarez died 1766
2 *See E.K.W.* 601
3 *See E.K.W.* 688

The documents descended in the Unwin family and were sold after the death of Captain Edward Unwin, V.C., in 1950 at Messrs. Sotheby (26th July, 1950), Six of the letters Nos. 82, 83, 85, 86, 90 and 92 and six drafts for payment Nos. 93—98 are now in the British Museum and include one draft not published by Harrison, that to Samuel Kilderbee (Pl. 25). The present whereabouts of the remaining documents are unknown.

See *K. W. Gransden,* British Museum Quarterly, *Vol. XX, 1956, pp. 59–60. The British Museum letters and the drafts are taken from the original manuscripts, the others from the* Connoisseur

82. TO JAMES UNWIN

Dear Sir, You must think me very unworthy of the sincere regard which your kind Letter proves you to have for me, to let it remain so long unanswered; and such I should certainly think myself, had not my absence from home been the cause of it. I had an unexpected call to London from whence I am but just returned. I had the pleasure of seeing your Brother for 5 minutes and fully intended to have spent a grave Evening with him, but such is the nature of that D—— place, or such that of this T.G. that I declare I never made a journey to London that I ever did what I intended. 'Tis a shocking place for *that* and I wonder amongst the number of things I leave undone which should be done, that I don't do many more which ought not to be done. I am going to settle in prodigiously hard to work and if you will be so good to divert Capt Saumarez[1] in the most ingenious way you can so that he will not fancy the time long before he has Mrs. Saumarez's Picture[2], I will endeavour *in the mean time* to make the *same* in reallity as short as possible.

But My Dear Friend how shall I continue with you concerning Mrs. Unwin's Picture.[3] I pray Sir, could not you *divert yourself* with the original for one week longer! I hope Mrs. Unwin is not so round but that you can bring that about. Pray make our joint Compliments to Her. Molly is better I think than ever she was, & the Captain *the same*

I am
Dear Sir Your most Affectionate
& Obliged humble servant
THO. GAINSBOROUGH

Bath, July 24th 1763

P.S.—I am much obliged for your care of my Note; are you sure it was paid?

My Dear Friend

Excuse my answering your Letter a little longer, for I am but just able to hold a Pen, and not able to know well what I say to you. I have kept my Bed 5 weeks to morrow excepting two hours sitting up for the last 3 Days of a most terrible Fever. It has been all upon my spirits from the *first*, that is from a single trip I made in London, as you guess'd; and occasioned by the uncertainty which followed the foolish Act. I was safe in the Opinion of two of the best men in their way, but possess'd in my Mind that I was ruin'd. O my dear Friend nobody can think what I have suffered for a moments gratification.

My life was dispair'd of by Doctor Charleton after he had tried all his skill, and by his own desire Dr. Moisey was call'd in when in three days my faintings left me and I got strength. I am now what they call out of Danger; I wish my Dear Friend I could sleep refreshing sleeps, then all would be well again. You shall hear from me again soon. My Dear Good Wife has set up every night ti'l within a few and has given me all the Comfort that was in her power. I shall never be a quarter good enough for her if I mend a hundred degrees.

Keep my secret, but remember us kindly to good Mrs. Unwin and believe me

Yrs most affectionately

ti'l Death

THO. GAINSBOROUGH

Bath 25th Oct⁰· 1763

My Dear Friend,—This is the first time I have been able to hold a pen since I wrote to you before. I have had a most terrible attack of a Nervous Fever so that for whole nights together I have thought it impossible that I could last 'til the morning.

But, thank God, I am greatly recover'd by the care and tenderness of Doctor Charlton who apply'd the Bark and Saline Draughts so properly and cautiously that they have done wonders, 'tho I must not forget a prescription of my sisters (who you know is a Woman of Courage) of six glasses of good old Port which she made me swallow one Evening when I should have thought two only must have knocked me off the Stage. The truth is, I have apply'd a little too close for these last 5 years, that both my Doctors and Friends really think.

1 Sir William St. Quintin, Fourth Baronet (1700–70), *see E.K.W.* 595

1 Miss Ford; became the third wife of Philip Thicknesse, *see p.* 144. She was a fan painter and an amateur musician who fancied herself on the Viol da Gamba. Her portrait by Gainsborough is now at the Art Museum, Cincinnati, *see E.K.W.* 660. In the British Museum is a drawing (*Pl.* 23) connected with the portrait

I have got a Horse which I had of my good friend Sir William St. Quintin,[1] not handsom but perfectly sure footed and steady upon the Road, and what I purpose is to be as indolent as possible in everything but observing the exact quantity of food and Exercises best for me, and to stick to the 6 glasses of Port at night. By this means I shall weather the Point, and live to see you at Bath and Mrs. Unwin who we should rejoyce to hear is well.

But all this time what is to be said about the Picture? I think I'll defer that 'til my next, for my Head throbs a little with writing, so my Dear Friend, Adieu for the present

and believe me, Yours most

sincerely and Affectionately

THO. GAINSBOROUGH

85. TO JAMES UNWIN

Dear Sir

I received yours with very great pleasure as I really began to fear that your Nerves were bad too not hearing from you—come I hope we shall do very well yet, I never had better spirits in all my life than I have now; I'm certainly repriev'd for this time & have got a new Lease. It has been of service to me, my Friend; I think better and will act better for the future. You have my sincerest thanks for your kind offer and intention in regard to Molly; but you must know I'm upon a scheme of learning them both to paint Landscape, and that somewhat above the common Fan mount stile. I think them capable of it, if taken in time, and with proper pains bestow'd. I don't mean to make them only Miss Fords[1] in the Art, to be partly admired & partly laugh'd at at every Tea Table; but in case of an Accident that they may do something for Bread.

You know it will be an Employment not so apt to lay snares in their way as Portrait or Miniature Painting, because they may be retired. I think (and indeed always did myself) that I had better do this than make fine trumpery of them, and let them be led away with Vanity, and ever subject to disappointment in the wild Goose chase. I've mark'd the end of it sufficiently. I'm in earnest and shall set about it in good earnest. My House, my dear Sir, brings me in the rent, with the expense I have been put at in Furniture; so make yourself easey, and you'l see this affair has been only the wag of a Dog's tail out of the strait Road: I may say I have already receiv'd more than

Plate 23
MISS FORD, AFTERWARDS MRS. PHILIP THICKNESSE
British Museum

Plate 24

GENERAL HONEYWOOD
Ringling Museum, Sarasota, U.S.A.

1 Probably *E.K.W.* 506

1 Gainsborough must often have visited Wilton, and made a copy from memory of the Van Dyck portrait of the Pembroke family, *see E.K.W.* 1015. It was at this time that his work began to be influenced by that of Van Dyck.

2 General Honeywood (*Pl.* 24) probably painted in 1764, now in the Ringling Museum, Sarasota, U.S.A., *see E.K.W. p.* 375

the expenses of it, having painted a whole length, three half lengths
and seven Heads, exclusive of a full length of Doctor Charleton, and a
half length of Doctor Moysey's son[1]. This is true my Friend 'tho. I am
so well known at Baddow. They know my Faults, but ask them *who*
knows any of my Virtues. Ah! that a Jackass should be so foolish.
You give us pleasure in the account of Mrs. Unwin and yourself
being well, and your intention of seeing Bath next Winter, but you
say nothing of your Son, so we conclude He is well too.

May we all continue so 'ti'l we have the pleasure of seeing you
here, you'l find me happy with old Marg^t I hope, and [much?]
yours

THO. GAINSBOROUGH

Landsdown Road

    March 1st 1764

I hope you are happily & situated in the House you mention,
which my Wife knows extremely well. Remember me kindly as the
Country folk say to Mrs. Itchener. She is a good little woman as ever
existed to my certain knowledge

Adieu I'm going
down to Bath.

Zouns I forgot Mrs. Unwin's & Capt. Saumarez's Picture. I shall
work upon them soon depend on't, that's enough.
Mr. Gainsborough 1st March 64

86. TO JAMES UNWIN, ESQ., AT BADDOW, NEAR CHELMSFORD, ESSEX

Dear Sir I was very agreeably favour'd with yours at my return
from Wilton[1] where I have been about a week, partly for my amusement, and partly to make a Drawing from a fine Horse of Ld.
Pembroke's, on which I am going to set General Honeywood,[2] as
large as life. We are extreemly glad to hear you and Mrs. Unwin are
pretty well. My wife says you goe on briskly. I tell her you was always
a brisk little man.

Thank God I have got the better of all my Complaints both real
& imaginary: I don't remember to have enjoy'd better health &
spirits any part of my life than at present. With regard to your
Baddow Friends, when you hear them touch my Character, you
may assure yourself that they attempt a thing as ridiculous to the full,
as if I undertook to draw their Pictures without ever having seen
them, for they know nothing of me. That you know the worst of me,
I am not sorry for, because I know you have good sense and good
nature to place things in their proper light; that they have either of

those blessings, who held me up to be view'd by you and Mrs. Unwin (who for ought they knew might have been strangers to me) is not quite so clear: however my Wife's compliments attend Mrs. H.

The Beauties of Mrs. Unwin's drapery like *our Virtues* have laid conceal'd for some time only to flash out the more suddenly, and to suprize those who least expect them. God bless you

I shall rejoyce to see you again at Bath—and am most sincerely Yours

THO. GAINSBOROUGH

My wife, Molly and the Capt. desire their respectful Compts. to you and Mrs. Unwin.

87. TO JAMES UNWIN

My Dear Friend,—My Head is so extreemly bad still, that 'tho' I have intended writing to you every day almost since the receipt of your last kind Letter, I have not been able to sit down 'til now. I have so many returns of my Nervous complaint in the back part of my Head, that I almost dispair of getting the better of it. I am really a weather cock; more so now than what you always took me for. All my hopes are built upon what the spring may do in throwing out the humour that yet seems playing about me. My spirits are at times so low, but damn it, I won't entertain you with any more of my misfortunes. We are sincerely glad that Mrs. Unwin is well, and wish you Joy of your son. I have taken a House about three quarters of a mile in the Lansdown Road; 'tis sweetly situated and I have every convenience I could wish for; I pay 30 pounds per year, and so let off all my House in the smoake except my Painting Room and best parlour to show Pictures in. Am I right to ease myself of as much Painting work as the Lodgings will bring in. I think the scheeme a good one. I Ride every minute in the Day unless it rains pouring; and do intend when I can, to be down from eleven to one o'clock, in my office, but not a moment longer for the King. I think I shall do yet my Friend. Pray have you any thoughts of paying us a visit this year? I long to see you more than all my Relations, for not one of them *knows what you do*. I always thought you extreemly clever; but whether I have not made you more knowing than you could have been had I been a close cunning fellow, that I must leave. I always think one cannot be too open to sensible people nor too reserved to fools; nay I believe I should have blush'd to have confess'd that to an Ass, which I did to you, and so much for secrets. Don't be revengeful now and not let me hear from you of a Month; for I promise upon

This letter is now in the Institut Néerlandais, Paris.
1 *See* Letters to Duke of Bedford *pp.* 36 & 37

the little honour I have left in your esteem, to be punctual in answering your Letters for the future.

My wife and my dear Girls beg to be remembered to yourself and Mrs. Unwin. They are thank God charmingly well, and what's more (tho' I say it), good in grain.

Adieu my dear Friend, and believe me,

Yours most Affectionately,

THOS. GAINSBOROUGH

P.S.—I fully intend to mention something about Mrs. Unwin's Picture in my next. I had a Letter with nobody's Name to it, desiring his Wife's Picture might be finish'd and sent as soon as possible; sure it could not be honest Saumarez. I think when I recollect the way he wears his Hat in, it may possibly come from him. How does your Brother? I pay'd him an exceeding short Visit when I was in Town; sure he could not smoake what was the matter with me by my down looks: he has a quick eye, I can tell you, as well as somebody else, 'tho not so perfectly the command of it; I think he does not meet Eyes quite so steadily as yourself, but don't you tell him what I say. Oh, my poor Head.

Don't you think a Jackass three quarters asleep upon the ridge of a Bank undermined and mouldring away is very expressive of the happiness of not seeing danger?

Dec: 30th 1763

88. TO JAMES UNWIN, ESQ., AT BADDOW, NEAR CHELMSFORD, ESSEX

My Dear Friend,—I have much against my Inclination suffer'd two posts to pass without thanking you for you last obliging Letter. I am very busy now in preparing a large Picture for the Exhibition, and have been closely employ'd all this winter, and thank God successfully, tho' so little deserving. I am not without hopes of taking a trip to Baddow just to look at you, and to admire how you and Mrs. Unwin go on (which according to your Letter cannot but excite admiration in all Beholders, if not a small matter of Imitation). It will depend upon a scheem taking place with the Duke of Bedford, whom you must know I made an exceeding like head of (tho' I say it) and also of the Duchess and Lady Mary Fitzpatrick[1] this winter in Bath; and since that I had a letter to inform me that more work was cutting out for me, and to know If I would goe to Town to do it. This came but the same post with your Letter, and I have answered that tho' I have refused frequent Invitations to undertake large

Plate 25
MONEY ORDER FROM GAINSBOROUGH TO MR. BERTIE BURGH
British Museum

July 22d 1759   5

Sir

please to pay to Mr. Saml. Kilderbee or
Order ten Days after the date hereof the
Sum of Fifty pounds, and place it to the
Account of

£50   Accepted for Brd.   Sir your most humble Servt.
                    C.R.   Tho Gainsborough

To Bertie Bugh Esqr. in Castle yard Holborn
                                                London

for you, the first I did, while I shew to Mr. Bowen,
when he called. pray favor me with a line
& believe me   dear Sir yours most sincerely
Tho Gainsborough
Bath July 28th 1763

Plate 26
FRAGMENT OF A LETTER WITH SKETCH
K. E. D. Rawlins, Esq.

o

Pictures in Town, on account of my Ill Health, I cannot resist the honour of doing something for the Duke of Bedford productive of future advantages, let the present Inconvenience be what it will to me. Am I right? When I read your Letter to Old Margaret, there, said she, you find Mr. Unwin is so much of a Gentleman now, that he would not mention a word to know if Mrs. Unwin's Picture was finished, and you so much of a scrubb that you'l not get it done for him. Says I, My Dear, hem, My Dear, He always was a Gentleman, you know from the first of our acquaintance he was a Gentleman, but, but what you scrubb, said she, have not you been as long about a shaddow as he have been in making three substantial whole length figures. No, my Dear, not three, but two. Yes, Mr. Dolittle, I say three. Pray did not Mrs. Unwin goe away big from Bath the summer before your Illness, and did not she lay in when we came to live up the Hill about this time, of her first child, and then according to Mr. Unwin's Letter again in August, and now three months gone again; I say three you scrubb. Pray is all this true or not, Sir?

Molly and the Capt. are out at School and have been these 5 months, otherwise they would most certainly join with Old Margaret in best respects to you and Mrs. Unwin. I am afraid I was not quite in my senses when I writ my last Letter to you. I beg my Compliments to Mrs. Itchiner, and am, Dear Sir,

Yours most sincerely and affectionately,

THO. GAINSBOROUGH

Bath, Jan. 21st 1765

89. TO JAMES UNWIN

Dear Sir,—To convince you that you have never said anything amiss in any one of your Letters, give me leave to assure you that it would never be in your power to offend me even by telling me the worst of my Faults, as I should esteem any correction as a favor from Mr. Unwin. Few Friends have regard enough to do so good an office, let their sincerity be what it will, and perhaps none of mine, except yourself, the judgment to apply the proper manner of doing it. I should think it a very bad sign was I capable of taking anything ill from a Person of your sense and good Qualities: it would be scorning to look at Vandyke whilst conscious of being yet but a dauber. No sir, I'm not quite so far gone neither.

My Health is better than ever, and everything goes on to my wishes, except Mrs. Unwin's Picture and that stands still, still in my Painting Room, notwithstanding I have the greatest desire to finish

1 Gainsborough lived in Hatton Garden when in London in his early life

it; I have no oftener promised myself the Pleasure of sitting down to
it but some confounded ugly creature or other have pop'd their
Heads in my way and hindred me: I do positively intend to lock
myself up one day soon, and order myself to be gone a Journey
through Essex to Harwich but what I will do it for you.

We are heartily glad you go on so merrily; you put me in mind of
a little Fiddle that Giardini pick'd up here at Bath, which nobody
would think well of, because there was nobody who knew how to
bring out the tone of, and which (though somewhat undersized) in
his Hands produced the finest Music in the World: I believe Mrs.
Unwin has found out the exact place where to fix your sound-post.
. . . Our best Compliments attend her.

I am, My Dear Friend,

most truly and sincerely yours,

THO. GAINSBOROUGH

Bath, Nov. 7th 1765

P.S.—My dear Girls are at Chelsea. I send you two Letters of theirs
to see how prettily they can write.

90. TO JAMES UNWIN ESQ., WOOTON LODGE NEAR ASHBURN, DERBYSHIRE

My dear Friend,

If any of my sitters were to appear in half so bad a light as I'm
certain I must do in your & Mrs. Unwin's Eyes, I should make the
Devil of them. Ingratitude how ugly—repeated neglects how unpardonable—and yet to write to me so good naturedly; believe me
my dear Friend I'm most horribly ashamed of myself—come to see
you indeed—why what a sweet Irish Countenance you must suppose
me to have. I should blush if I thought you could ever spy me
through a Telescope within the distance of a whole County of you.
If the People with their damn'd Faces could but let me alone a little
I believe I should soon appear in a more tolerable light but I have
been plagued very much. Thank God I shall now shut myself up for
the summer and not appear til September comes in—methinks I
hear you say ay, or suppose you hang yourself up for the Summer and
the winter too—shall I never mend O dear O dear I don't think
I'm a bit altered since I lived in Hatton Garden[1] only that I'm
Grey in the Poll—my Wife says I am not so good as I was then tho
I take more pains. Well, I'm better settled tho than ever I was in my
Life, *more settled* more creditably settled and happier so who knows.
You don't say whether you are better in your Health nor how Mrs.
Unwin does—now I blush again. The weather Sir, is *settled* in very

This letter is now in the Institut Néerlandais, Paris.

1 George Pitt, first Lord Rivers (1721–1803), *see E.K.W.* 577 – *see* Letters to Jackson *p.* 123

2 Exhibited R.A. 1771, *see E.K.W.* 443 *and* 444

fine in these Parts but rather too warm for Riding in the middle of the day especially upon Lansdown where there is no shade.

I suppose your Country is very woody—pray have you Rocks and Waterfalls! for I am as fond of Landskip as ever. The Captain begs her Comp^ts only she is making a damned jangling upon the Harpsicord this moment. Molly and Mam: also desires their best respects thank God they are well and too *good for* [letter torn] but says you again why I know that [letter torn] do know a good deal I must confess but still I desyre you to be certain how much I really am

Your affectionate & sincere

obed^t Servt

Bath May 25th, 1768   THO. GAINSBOROUGH

God bless that good woman Mrs. Somerez.

Don't you come to Bath this year! pray let me hear from you soon.

Could I send a case cross the Country to you, or best by London.

91. TO JAMES UNWIN, ESQ., AT WOOTON LODGE,
NEAR ASHBURN, DERBYSHIRE

My Dear Friend,—Ever since the receipt of your last *undeserv'd* favor, I have been tossed about like a ship in a storm: I went by appointment only to spend two or three Days at Mr. George Pitt's[1] Country House, by way of taking leave of him, as a staunch Friend of mine before his going to Spain, and behold he had got two whole length canvasses, and his son and daughter, *Lord & Lady Ligonier*,[2] in readiness to take me prisoner for a month's work—you'l say I might have wrote to you from thence, and so I certainly should but that I left your Letter at home, and forgot your direction. It may seem very odd, and I'll lay fifty pounds you'l think 'tis a d——m'd lie, but the D——l fetch me if I have been able to direct a Letter to you these 5 years, owing to your removal from Essex.

I have been just going to write to your Brother many times for your direction, but have been always prevented by the curs'd Face Business— If you'l believe me, my Dear Friend, there is not a man in the World who has less time to call his own, and that would so willingly spend some of it in the enjoyment of an Old Acquaintance. My Regard for you was originally built upon such a foundation that you know no time can shake, nor ought not; but the nature of face painting is such, that if I was not *already cracked*, the continual hurry of one fool upon the back of another, just when the magot bites, would be enought to drive me crazy. Let us, for an experiment try what a renewal of our Acquaintance would do towards making me

behave well for the future; you say if I would come and see you in Derbyshire, you w'd return our Visit to Bath. By G——, if you will come *this Autumn* and bring Mrs. Unwin for six weeks, and make our house your home, I'll pack up all my Drawing things, and see Derbyshire next summer, if I'm alive. What say you? Let us be at a word now.

I'm so ashamed to mention Mrs. Unwin's Picture that D——m me, I wish I was a Razor-grinder—I'll begin a new one of Her and you together if you'l come. Poor Mrs. Saumarez too, O Lord—that I should behave worst to my best friends and best to my worst—I hate myself for this, tho' even my Enemies say I have some good qualities. If there is any one Devil uglier than another, 'tis the appearance of Ingratitude join'd to such a Face as mine. Let me before I get more out of patience with myself, tell you that my Wife and Daughters desire their best Respects to yourself and Mrs. Unwin; and hope you'l agree to my proposal.

Believe me, Dear Sir, Yours Affectionately,

THO. GAINSBOROUGH

Bath, July 10th 1770

92. TO JAMES UNWIN, ESQ., AT WOOTON PARK, NEAR ASHBURN, DERBYSHIRE

My dear Friend

The reason and only reason I did not answer your last obliging Letter was that just at the time I received it, a Lady, her son and servants arrived at our house upon a long invitation from my Wife whose acquaintance she is, to stay at our House; this you may guess was a pleasant circumstance as I was about to appoint a time for our pleasure of seeing you and Mrs. Unwin; I have been ever since harkening to the time of her intention of going that I might answer your Letter, but behold (owing to warm intreaties from some part (not the most insignificant of my Family) she now proposes to spend her Chrismas here. We never had above a Bed & a half to spare in our lives, and so I am reduced to offer my Friendship only to take Lodgings for you according to your directions, if you favor me with them. I am sorry to hear that Bath waters have any part in the occasion of your coming; I hope we shall ride often together, and set you up for another seven years

Believe me

Dear Sir (with all our joint Comp^{ts} to

Mrs. U & self

Yours most truly

Bath

THO. GAINSBOROUGH

Nov 15th. 1770

170   93. *Draft for payment to Mrs. Ann Christian.*

Bath Decemb^{r} 31st 1759

Sir
       Please to pay to Mrs. Ann Christian or Order three weeks after
the Date hereof the sum of Thirty pounds, and place it to the
account
                              of Sir Your most Obed. humb.
                       Servt
                              THOS. GAINSBOROUGH
To Mr. James Unwin
       Castle Yard Holborn Lond
              Acc. Jan: 5, 1759 ju
                       [Signed]
       Witnes Chas Turner   Ann Christian

94. *Draft for payment to Michael Thirkle, Esq.*

8/11 August
                                              June 27th 1758
Sir
       Please to pay to Mich^{le} Thirkle Esqr. or Order six weeks after
the Date hereof the sum of Ten pounds and place it to the acc^{t}. of
                              Sir
£10   Your most hum^{b} Servt.
                              THO. GAINSBOROUGH
To Mr. James Unwin in Castle
Yard Holborn, London—
              Accepted July 17th 1758
              J. Unwin.

95. *Draft for payment to Mrs. Ann Christian.*

Jan: 28th 1758
Sir
       Please to pay to Mrs. Ann Christian or order a month after
Date hereof the sum of forty nine pounds ten shillings, and place
it to the acc^{t} of Sir
                       Your most Obed^{t} humble Ser^{t}
£49. 10.   THO. GAINSBOROUGH
To Bertie Burgh Esq. in Castle
Yard Holborn Lond^{n}

2 Aug.^t

July 10th 1758

Sir,

Please pay to Mrs. John Fowler or order twenty days after Date, the sum of sixty seven pounds sixteen shils and place it to the acc.^t of

Sir your most humb^{le} Servt

THO. GAINSBOROUGH

£67. 16
Accepted 13th July 1758
        J. Unwin
To Mr. James Unwin in Castle
Yard Holborn London

97. *Draft for payment to Mr. Nathaniel Burrough.*

July 3.rd 1758

Sir

Please to pay to Mr. Nath^{le} Burrough or order a month after the Date hereof the sum of Ten pounds and place it to the account
        of Sir your most obed.^t Ser.^t

THO. GAINSBOROUGH

£10
To Mr. James Unwin in Castle
Yard & Holborn Lond
Accepted 13th July 1758
        J. Unwin

98. *Draft for payment to Mr. Samuel Kilderbee (Pl. 25).*

July 22nd 1757

Sir,

Please to pay to Mr Sam^{le} Kilderbee or Order ten Days after the Date hereof the Sum of fifty pounds, and place it to the
        Account of
£50   Accepted for Bro.   Sir your most humb^{le} Servt
        C.N.   THOS. GAINSBOROUGH
To Bertie Burgh Esqr in Castle yard Holborn
        London

172

From the Historical MS. Commission, Ninth Report, *p.* 481, as in the collection of Alfred Morrison

1 William Sharp (1749–1824) engraved a portrait of John Hunter by Sir Joshua Reynolds

From the original in the collection of K. E. D. Rawlins, Esq., *Pl.* 26

99. NO ADDRESSEE

It is my strict charge that after my decease no plaster cast, model, or likeness whatever be permitted to be taken: But that if Mr. Sharp,[1] who engraved Mr. Hunter's print, should choose to make a print from the $\frac{3}{4}$ sketch, which I intended for Mr. Abel, painted by myself, I give free consent.

THO. GAINSBOROUGH

June 15th 1788

100. FRAGMENT WITH A DRAWING NO ADDRESSEE

of something better. I have sent you two bottles of Varnish, of my own making, so that if you like it I can either give you more of the same or a Rect how to make it You are to lay on . . .
for you, the first I did, which I shew to Mr. [Bolding?] when he called. pray favor me with a Line & believe me

Dear Sir yours most sincerely

THO. GAINSBOROUGH

Bath July 28th 1763

Extracts from letter sold at Sotheby's, 23rd July, 1962 (284)
Postmarked 1 *April : Bath* (probably 1773)

1 John Henderson. See biographical note on page 92

2 Gainsborough quarrelled with the Academy about the hanging of his pictures, and did not send to the exhibitions between 1773 and 1777, *see Whitley p.* 96.

Extract from letter sold at Sotheby's, 23rd July, 1962 (285)

1 Nathaniel Dance (1735–1811), associated with Gainsborough in disagreement with the Academy in 1773. He exhibited Garrick as Richard III in 1771.

101. TO DAVID GARRICK

   . . . for my own part, I think he[1] must be your Bastard. He is absolutely a Garrick through a Glass not quite drawn to its focus, a little mist hangs about his outlines, and a little fuzziness in the tone of his voice, otherwise the very ape of all your tricks, and by G—— exceedingly sensible, humble & diffident—how like you then must he be . . .

   . . . O that I could but touch his features, clean his Person, & sharpen him out into a real Garrick. Face, Person & Voice, have fallen to the share of no *one* Genius but yourself my Friend. Many as great a Genius has been hang'd, but only yourself bless'd with every requisite to the last minute touch, so as to show us *Perfection.* I'm sure it must please you to see the same thing short of you, whenever you choose to turn your head back, as the Jockeys do when they are near the Post . . . I don't send to the Exhibition this year; they hang my likenesses too high to be seen, & have refused to lower one sail to oblige me . . .

102. TO DAVID GARRICK

   . . . Had I dreamt that it w^d: have afforded the least satisfaction to my good Friend that I should have poked my long neck and hatchet Face into his doors, in the common how d'e do way, not all the Giardini's on Earth should have prevented me; but I did not know that a first Man, assured of the affection as well as admiration of all sorts and sizes, expected every common hack to interrupt Him in his precious Moments . . .

   Well, we did not make ourselves, if we had by G—— you with all your Genius, could not have made anything half so clever as a Garrick, tho he is not music-mad—you pretend in your clever mixture of Love & Abuse in Palmer's Letter, to flatter me with the notion that if I had call'd Mrs. Garrick should have sat to me for a Picture, that's all a D——md L—— for you'd let Dance[1] or anybody cleverer than I, sooner than put such a Feather in my cap . . . May God preserve you . . . long amongst your Admirers; for no man will be left behind with even Genius enough to imagine what sort of a creature that little diamond of a Man was . . .

Bath 24 March 1774

From the original letter in the possession of Mr. Norman Plaistow, A.R.I.B.A., Coach House, Wimbledon

This letter explains Gainsborough's technique for his varnished drawings, which has always been something of a puzzle, since the white touches have a dry appearance, resembling chalk rather than oil paint. According to the letter this seems to be due to the use of Bristol chalk, used in an ingenious way.

Dear Jackson of Exeter

There is not a man living that you can mention (besides *yourself* and one more, living) that shall ever know my secret of making those studies you mention—I have a real regard for you, and would tell you anything except one [word erased, fact ?] in the world & that shall die with me.

You may acquaint your Friend that you tried your strength with me for the secret, but the *fixing the white chalk* previous to tinging the Drawing with waterColors, you find I am determined never to tell to anybody; and here you'l get off, for no Chalk is used, and so keep it close for your own use; and when you can make a Drawing to please your self by my direction send it to me, & I'll tell you if they are right.

Mind now—take half a sheet of blotting paper such as the Clerks and those that keep books put upon writing instead of sand; 'tis a spongy purple paper, paste that and half a sheet of white paper, of the same size, together, let them dry, and in that state keep them for use—take a Frame of deal about two Inches larger every way, and paste, or glue, a few sheets of very large substantial paper, no matter what sort, thick brown, blue, or any; then cut out a square half an Inch less than the size of your papers for Drawing; so that it may serve for a perpetual stretcing Frame for your Drawings; that is to say after you have dipt your drawing as I shall by & by direct in a liquid, in that wet state you are to take, and run some hot glue and with a brush run round the border of your stretcher, gluing about half an Inch broad, which is to receive your half an Inch extra-ordinary allow'd for that purpose in your drawing paper, so that when that dries, it may be like a drum. Now before you do anything by way of stretching, make the black and white of your drawing, the Effect I mean, and disposition in rough, Indian Ink shadows & your lights of *Bristol* made *white lead* which you buy in lumps at any house painters; saw it the size you want for your white chalk; the Bristol is harder and more the temper of chalk than the London. When you see your effect, dip it all over in skim'd milk; put it wet on your Frame just glued as before observed let it dry; and then you correct your Effects with Indian Ink when dry & if you want to add more lights or alter, do it and dip again, til all your effect is to your mind; then tinge in your greens, your browns with sap green & Bistre, your yellows with Gall stone & blues with fine Indigo [word illegible]— when this is done, float it all over with Gum water, 3 ounces of Gum Arabic to a pint of water with a Camels pencil let that dry & varnish

From the original in the possession of Mr. and Mrs. Paul Mellon
Probably written in 1753 and therefore the earliest known letter

1 Gainsborough's landlady in Ipswich from 1752–59, *see Whitley pp.*22 *and* 26

2 Vernon, Admiral Edward (1684–1757); he bought Nacton in Suffolk and became M.P. for Ipswich. The portrait now in the National Portrait Gallery, London, was probably painted about 1753, *see Whitley p.*12

From the original in the possession of Mr. and Mrs. Paul Mellon.

From the original in the possession of the Marquess of Lansdowne. (I am indebted to Miss Polly Eccles for bringing this letter to my notice.)

1 Later, 1st Marquess of Lansdowne (1737–1805). Painted by Gainsborough in 1787 reported to be as a present for the King of France, *see Whitley pp.* 271–272. The portrait is only known from the stipple engraving by Bartolozzi, *see E.K.W.* 428

2 Bartolozzi, Francesco (1727–1815), engraver, born Florence, came to England 1764, a foundation member of the Royal Academy. Best known for his engravings after the Italian Masters and Holbein

it 3 times with spirit varnish such as I sent you; tho only Mastic & Venice Turpentine is sufficent, then cut out your drawing but observe it must be varnished both sides to keep it flat trim it round with a pen knife & Ruler, and let any body produce the like if they can; stick them upon a white paper leaving a Margin of an Inch and half round.

Swear now never to impart my secret to any one living—
Yours sincerely
THO. GAINSBOROUGH

Bath Jan 29th 1773.

104. TO MRS. RASSE[1]

Madam

I call'd yesterday upon a Friend in hopes of borrowing money to pay you, but was disappointed & as I shall finish the Admiral's picture in a week you shall have it when I go to Nacton, will call & pay you[2] at your new abode.

I'm sorry it happens so but you know I cant make money any more than yourself & when I receive it you shall surely have it before anybody.

Who am
Mad^m Yours to Com^d
THO. GAINSBOROUGH

Thursday morning

105. *Receipt for rent*

April 1760 by the order of Mr Gainsborough R^d of Mr. Mils five pounds Ten Shillings fr Half a year Rent. Due at a Lady Last
p. Eliz Rasse

106. TO WILLIAM, LORD SHELBURNE[1]

My Lord,

Mr. Bartolozzi[2] has this day favour'd me with the print of your Lordship; and I could wish he had favor'd me a little more in preserving your Lordships chearful countenance—It wants (in my humble opinion, *a full Bottle of Champagne* to give even the Vigour that is in the picture, and *that* falls as short as dead small Beer of the original—I beg pardon my Lord, but I'm in a damn'd passion about it, because I have ever been so partial to Bartolozzi's work—He has

The two following letters are addressed to Henry Briggs by Sir George Beaumont and refer to a copy of Jackson's character of Gainsborough. Henry Perronet Briggs (?1791–1844) was a painter and a friend of Margaret Gainsborough when they were neighbours at Acton; she left to him a number of her father's pictures, *see Whitley unpublished papers, British Museum*. The letters together with other objects descended in the Briggs family and finally came into the possession of Mr. Phillips Hill, a member of the famous firm of violin makers, who presented the letters and a deed poll signed by Margaret Gainsborough to the City Museum & Art Gallery, Birmingham

mounted your Lordship's figure up to about Lord Stormont's height, and sloped the shoulders like *my layman* stuff'd with straw; which he need not have done in order to bring into that size oval, as he might have taken the Head larger: but what hurts me most is that the Head is long instead of round—why will Bartolozzi, my Lord, spend his last precious moments in f———g a young Woman, instead of out doing all the world with a Graver; when perhaps all the world can outdo Him at the former work!

Pray My Lord apply these private hints as from your own eyes, lest I should have my throat cut for my honesty—

Your Lordships most obediant,

Humble Servant

THO. GAINSBOROUGH

107. FROM SIR GEORGE BEAUMONT TO HENRY BRIGGS

Dear Sir

As I was prevented having the pleasure of calling at Acton before I left town I have frequently reproached myself for not having written to thank you again for your uncommon attention. But having just read over the extract from Jacksons life of Gainsborough, which you were kind enough to take so much pains in transcribing for me, I can no longer pardon myself for the neglect. With regard to the extract I must confess I think it very unfair both in criticism & in personal remark. I know not that any personal pique prevailed between them, but it is unjust to him as an Artist, & seems intended to make him ridiculous as a man. No man who knew Gainsborough as I had the pleasure to know him could possibly imagine him capable of such folly as he accuses him of respecting musical instruments— fond of them he certainly was, & took great pains to buy the best, & would give large prices for them.—He offered any picture he had to a friend of mine for a fiddle—But in that case at least he could not have been tempted by the harmonious tones brought forth by my friend, & been absurd enough to suppose the merit in the instrument altogether, & that it would enable him to do the same but my friend was a very indifferent performer, yet Gainsborough saw it was an excellent fiddle & very rationally thought it would enable him to make the best use of his own skill—I will venture to say that Jackson himself was not more above such ridiculous weakness—yet I have much respect for Jackson's Genius in his own line, but I have a still higher respect for the powers of Gainsborough in his. As a painter Jackson was below mediocrity, at least as far as I can judge by the

works of his which I have seen—But I am giving you more trouble than I intended, which I hope you will excuse & believe me to be

Dear Sir

Your faithful

& obliged servant

G. H. BEAUMONT

I shall take the liberty to send a little game to Acton which I hope will be acceptable & arrive safe. As I am not quite sure of your address may I request the favour of a line.

Cole-Orton Hall, Ashby de la Zouch, Nov 11th 1829

108. FROM SIR GEORGE BEAUMONT TO HENRY BRIGGS

Dear Sir,

I gave directions to my servant the other day to send you a hare and a pheasant, but I am sorry to find he neglected to pay the carriage, this is not my usual practice, I hope you will excuse it, it shall not happen again.

If it appeared by my letter I meant to say Jackson wilfully falsified the character of Gainsborough, I did not express my opinion as I intended, Jackson was unquestionably a man of Genius & I dare say above such an intention. I think he was deceived either by his own prejudices or by the prejudices of others. But whatever was the cause I think no one who knew Gainsborough well could have thought him capable of such folly.

The compliment you pay me by wishing for another essay of mine is very encouraging especially when I know with what pictures you are surrounded but in fact I have given away very few pictures, not from an opinion of their value but I can assure you I seldom produce one which I can comfortably give away lest it should rise up in judgement against me, nevertheless, you have been so very obliging that, I should be fortunate to satisfy myself in a tolerable degree. I shall with pleasure present one to you, but observe I do not promise, I am already deeply in debt, & must not add to the weight of my obligations—In the meantime will you favour me with the size of the sketch you already have, of which you have made me so excellent a memorandum.

I am dear Sir

Your obliged Servant

C. H. BEAUMONT

Cole-Orton Hall,
Nov. 30 1829.

INDEX TO LETTERS

*The Letters are arranged alphabetically according to the names of the recipients;
as many are undated a chronological sequence is impossible.*